Egypt

Egypt

BY ANN HEINRICHS

Enchantment of the World
Second Series

Children's Press®

A Division of Grolier Publishing

NEW YORK   LONDON   HONG KONG   SYDNEY
DANBURY, CONNECTICUT

Consultant: Terence P. Moran, Ph.D., Professor of Culture and Communication, School of Education, New York University, and Chairman, Board of Directors, American Egyptian Cooperation Foundation

Please note: All statistics are as up-to-date as possible at the time of publication.

Library of Congress Cataloging-in-Publication Data

Heinrichs, Ann.
       Egypt / Ann Heinrichs.
       p. cm. — (Enchantment of the world. Second series)
       Includes bibliographical references (p.) and index.
Summary: Describes the geography, plants, animals, history, economy, language, religions, culture, sports, arts, and people of Egypt.
       ISBN 0-516-20470-X
       1. Egypt—Juvenile literature. [1. Egypt.] I. Title. II. Series
       DT49.H45 1997
       962—dc21   97-2438
                                                     CIP
                                                       AC

Acknowledgments

I am grateful to Martha and Magdy Farahat for their hospitality, kindness, and crisis management during my stay in Egypt; to Egyptologist Manal Helmy for giving me a grand tour of all of Egyptian history and culture; and to Danny Brady and Wayne Redmond of Imaginative Traveller for making sure my trip was the ultimate in education, hardship, and fun.

Contents

Cover photo:
Silhouettes on the
Giza plateau

Egypt's Western Desert

Things of Unspeakable Greatness

Fourteen-year-old Karima blushed as she removed her veil in the schoolyard. "I had no choice," she said. The school principal had told her to take it off or be expelled.

KARIMA AND HER FAMILY ARE STRICT MUSLIMS. LIKE many other Egyptians, they follow the rules of their Islamic faith closely. Under Islamic law, girls and women are required to dress modestly. But the government had just banned the *niqab*—a veil that reveals only the eyes—in public schools.

Across the country, parents hired lawyers to argue their daughters' right to wear the veil. However, Egypt's highest court ruled that schoolgirls' uniforms were modest enough to meet with Islamic principles.

Cairo schoolchildren on the way home from school

Karima's predicament is typical of a problem in her country today. Egypt is torn by opposing ideals. One tradition stresses openness, tolerance, and diversity. The other insists on one belief and one way of observing religious teachings.

In spite of their disagreements, however, Egyptians are more alike than they are different. Arabic culture permeates their everyday lives. They share Arabic language, music, art, festivals, and food. In their reli-

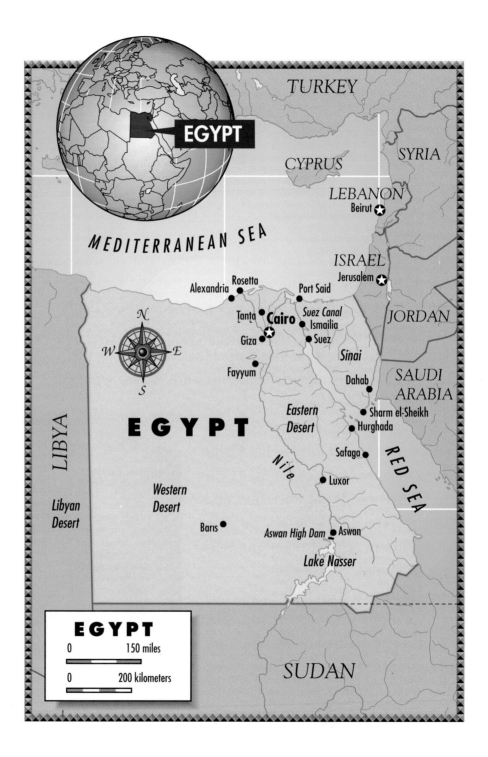

Geopolitical map
of Egypt

gion, too, Egyptians find a sense of community that runs deeper than their differences.

Egyptians also share a pride in their ancient heritage. Almost 2,500 years ago, the Greek historian Herodotus visited Egypt. He was astonished by what he saw. "Nowhere are there so many marvelous things," he wrote, "nor in the whole world are there to be seen so many things of unspeakable greatness."

Ancient Egyptians developed one of the earliest civilizations on earth. How did they build their fabulous pyramids, temples, and tombs? We may never know. Even with modern, high-tech equipment, most of these monuments would be impossible to build today.

In Egypt's Valley of the Kings, a laborer digs out a newly discovered tomb. It is a dirty, backbreaking job in the sweltering desert sun. When a visitor asks how he feels about his task, the young man smiles proudly.

"I am descended from the people who built this tomb," he replies. "I can feel their blood is in me."

This is an aerial view of the Great Pyramid, the largest Giza pyramid, located near the Great Sphinx.

Black Land, Red Land

Egypt is a desert with a river running through it. About 96 percent of Egypt's land is desert, but the life-giving Nile, the longest river in the world, flows between its Western and Eastern Deserts. Ancient Egyptians called their land *Kemet*, meaning "Black Land," for the rich soil of the Nile River Valley. *Deshret*, the Red Land, was the surrounding desert.

EGYPT COVERS AN AREA ALMOST AS LARGE AS THE U.S. states of Texas and New Mexico combined. It is slightly larger than the Canadian province of British Columbia. Add a north-south view to this image. Upper Egypt and the Upper Nile are in the south, where the land is higher. Lower Egypt and the Lower Nile are in the north.

Nearly all of Egypt is in the continent of Africa. The Sinai Peninsula, which lies in Egypt's northeast corner beyond the Suez Canal, is the only part of Egypt that lies in Asia. The Suez Canal marks the dividing line between the two continents.

The Deserts

Egypt's two largest land regions are the Western Desert and the Eastern Desert. The Western Desert, also called the Libyan Desert, covers about two-thirds of the country. It is part of northern Africa's great Sahara Desert, extending west into Libya and south into Sudan.

A wind-eroded mushroom rock in the Western Desert

Topographical map of Egypt

Geographical Features

Highest Elevation: *Jabal Katrinah* (Mount Saint Catherine), 8,651 feet (2,637 m)

Lowest Elevation: Qattara Depression, 436 feet (133 m) below sea level

Largest City: Cairo

Lowest Average Temperature: Giza, 55°F (13°C) (January)

Highest Average Temperature: Aswan, 92°F (33°C) (June)

Lowest Annual Rainfall *(excluding the desert)*: Aswan, 0.1 inch (0.25 cm)

Longest River: The Nile, 4,145 miles (6,670 km) (longest in the world)

Largest Lake: Lake Nasser, largest artificial lake in the world

World's First Inter-Ocean Shipping Canal: Suez Canal, completed in 1869

World's Largest Monuments: The Great Pyramids at Giza

The Western Desert is a vast expanse of rippling sand, blown by ever-shifting winds. Rocky ridges jut out here and there, and in some places, the sand piles up to form graceful dunes. The desert sands can be destructive, however, when they blow over farmlands and villages. The Qattara Depression, a sunken area in the north, is Egypt's lowest point.

The Eastern Desert is also called the Arabian Desert. Long ago, before the Red Sea existed, it was joined to the Arabian Peninsula. From the east bank of the Nile, the Eastern Desert slopes gently upward into rocky hills that line the seacoast. Deep ravines called *wadis* cut through the hills.

Few people live in the Eastern Desert, but several small towns lie along the coast. The northern coastal waters of Hurghada, the center for Egypt's Red Sea oil-drilling activities, are severely polluted. South of the town though, the water is clean enough to attract divers to explore the coast's spectacular coral reefs.

Egypt's Western Desert covers about two-thirds of the country's land area.

Near Rosetta, the Nile River joins the Mediterranean Sea.

Without the Nile River, Egypt would be one huge desert. But the Nile has nourished Egypt's farms for thousands of years. It flows through Egypt for almost 1,000 miles (1,600 km).

The waters of the Nile flow from two sources. Upstream in central Sudan, the White Nile and the Blue Nile join to form one river. The White Nile, the longer branch, rises in Burundi, deep in the heart of Africa. From there to the Mediterranean Sea, the Nile is 4,145 miles (6,670 km) long.

Most of the Nile's water, however, comes from the Blue Nile, which rises in the highlands of Ethiopia. The torrential summer rains there cause the annual floods in Egypt.

Near Cairo, Egypt's capital city, the Nile fans out into dozens of streams that empty into the Mediterranean. This sediment-rich area is named the Delta, after the Greek letter shaped like a triangle (Δ). The Delta stretches about 100 miles (160 km) from north to south and about 160 miles (258 km) along the coast. Almost all of Egypt's farmland is in the Delta and in

Looking at Egyptian Cities

Egypt's second-largest city, Alexandria (top), founded by Alexander the Great in 332 B.C., is a busy port on the Mediterranean Sea. Alexandria is the site of Qaytbey Fort, Pompey's Pillar, Kom al-Shogafa Catacombs, Anfushi and Chatby Tombs, Ras al-Tin Palace, Kom al-Dikka Amphitheater, and the Greco-Roman Museum.

A suburb of Cairo, Giza is the site of the Great Pyramids, the Great Sphinx, and the Solar Boat Museum.

One of Egypt's oldest cities, Luxor, was originally the ancient city of Thebes. Luxor is famous for its many temples and tombs, including the Luxor Temple and Museum (bottom left), the temple of Karnak, and the Valley of the Kings.

Founded in the 1860s during the building of the Suez Canal (bottom right), Port Said is one of Egypt's chief ports.

Lake Nasser, Egypt's largest lake, was created by the construction of the Aswan High Dam in the 1960s.

the narrow strip along the river. Most of Egypt's people live in these areas, too. Alexandria is a historic Delta city that sits right on the seacoast.

Western Desert Oases

An oasis is an area in the desert where water flows underground. In Western Desert oases, the water gushes up in springs and gathers into ponds and wells surrounded by tall date palms and lush gardens. In some oases, the underground waters feed rich, green valleys.

Oases closest to the Nile are called the New Valley oases—Bahariyah, Farafirah, Dakhilah, and Kharijah. Long ago, a branch of the Nile flowed through them. Other oases are Baris, south of Kharijah, and Siwa, near the Libyan border.

A large settlement called the Fayyum lies just west of the Nile. Its palm trees, mountains, and ancient ruins are surrounded by desert, but the Fayyum is not really an oasis. Its water supply comes from a tributary, or branch, of the Nile.

Oasis water, rich with sulphur and other minerals, is known for its health benefits. People come from all over the world to bathe in these waters. The silt—particles of sediment that sink to the bottom—is also used to treat bone, skin, muscle, and stomach problems.

Lake Nasser and the Aswan High Dam

Lake Nasser, south of Aswan, is Egypt's largest lake. It stretches for 312 miles (502 km) across Egypt's border into Sudan. Lake Nasser is an artificial lake created in the 1960s by building the Aswan High Dam across the Nile.

In the 1950s, President Gamal Abdel Nasser decided to build the Aswan High Dam. Waters building up behind the dam would form a lake, but that presented a problem. The lake would flood ancient monuments such as the Temples of Abu Simbel and Philae. Thousands of engineers and laborers from all over the world formed a "rescue team" to save them. Stone by stone, they moved

Before the Aswan High Dam was built, workers dismantled the temple of Abu Simbel and moved it to higher ground to prevent the structure from being flooded.

the monuments to higher ground. This massive project took over ten years. The Aswan High Dam and its power station began operating in 1968.

Damming the Nile has brought many benefits. It controls Egypt's annual floodwaters, enabling farmers to grow crops all year round, and it makes irrigation easier. Also, water rushing over the dam produces hydroelectric power and improves boat travel on the Nile.

The dam has its drawbacks, however. It traps silt from the river in Lake Nasser. The Nile Valley no longer gets that natural fertilizer. The Delta has suffered, too. Without the Nile's natural gushing force, salt water from the Mediterranean creeps upstream. And without steady silt deposits, the Mediterranean coast is eroding, or washing away.

Opposite: **Aswan High Dam**

The Colored Canyon in the Sinai, near Mount Sinai

The Sinai Peninsula

The Sinai Peninsula is part desert and part rocky mountains, an area with more camel trails than roads. Bedouin nomads have lived in the Sinai for centuries. Now, vacationers and tourists visit the seaside resort towns that line the Sinai's Mediterranean coast. Al-Arish, for example, once a small Bedouin village, is now the Sinai's largest city.

Rocky mountain ranges rise in the south. The best-known peaks are *Jabal Katrinah* (Mount Saint Catherine)—

Egypt's highest point—and *Jabal Musa* (Mountain of Moses or Mount Sinai). At the base of Mount Sinai is Saint Catherine's Greek Orthodox Monastery. The Colored Canyon, not far from Mount Sinai, has striped rock formations in shades of pink, orange, and yellow.

Southern Sinai is flanked by two arms of the Red Sea—the Gulf of Suez on the west and the Gulf of Aqaba on the east. Tourists enjoy south Sinai's coastal resort cities. Some are simple towns with thatched-roof waterfront huts, while others offer lavish hotels, restaurants, and entertainment. Snorkeling and scuba diving near the coral reefs are also major attractions.

Map of Egypt's vegetation

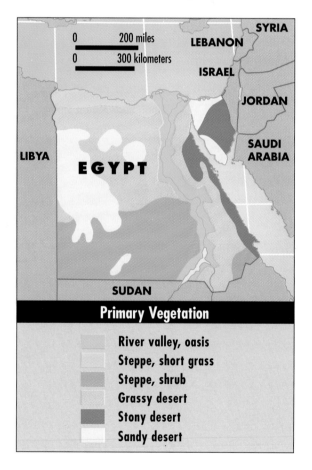

Primary Vegetation

River valley, oasis
Steppe, short grass
Steppe, shrub
Grassy desert
Stony desert
Sandy desert

Climate

Egypt has two seasons—summer and winter. Summers, from May through October, are sweltering. To escape the heat, many Egyptians head for the cool sea breezes of the Mediterranean coast. Winters—November through April—are mild and sometimes cool. All year long, temperatures in Upper Egypt are higher than those in the north. In the Sinai, mountainous regions can be quite chilly.

In the desert, the glaring sun makes midday travel dangerous. Camelback travelers sometimes sleep during the hottest part of the day. They travel before

The 1992 Earthquake

One of the worst earthquakes in Egypt's history occurred in October 1992. Registering 5.9 on the Richter scale, it struck the crowded Cairo area, killing almost 600 people. Many of the injured were children trapped in school.

mid-morning and after sundown. Nights in the desert, however, can be icy cold because sand does not retain the sun's heat. In April, desert dwellers take cover during the *khamsin*— a hot, dry wind from the south that causes blinding sandstorms.

Most of Egypt's rain falls in winter near the Mediterranean. It almost never rains in the desert. Snow is seen only on the Sinai's highest mountaintops where some 11 inches (28 cm) falls every year.

Creatures of the Desert, Water, and Sky

With its sweltering days and chilly nights, the desert is a rough habitat for animals. Skinks, lizards, and other reptiles can stand these extremes, but some animals, such as hyenas and mice, creep out only at night.

EGYPT'S TEMPLES AND PYRAMIDS MAKE SAFE HOMES FOR many animals. The monuments shelter them from the desert heat and provide good hiding places. Inside, colonies of bats cling to the ceilings and walls. The golden spiny mouse sleeps in a dark corner in the daytime and comes out at night. The orange head of the agama, or gray lizard, blends in with the stones. Rock martins and white-crowned wheatears build their nests in the nooks and crevices.

Many species prefer the wetlands. Long-legged herons and other wading birds feed on fish along the banks of the Nile, while lapwings soar overhead. Gulls, ospreys, and spoonbills nest on the Red Sea coast. Lake Nasser is a haven for migrating birds. Pelicans, geese, terns, plovers, and warblers are seen along the shore. Crocodiles, once honored as the god Sobek, slither along the banks.

Birds nesting in temple carvings

The ibex, a wild mountain goat with long, curved horns, scampers over steep, rocky slopes in the Sinai. In the daytime, a Sinai rodent called the rock hyrax basks in the sun. At night, it eats acacia plants.

Cattle egrets are a common sight in farming areas. They dip over the fields looking for insects and frogs. Doves, bee-eaters, and black kites live in the countryside as well as the cities. Hoopoes are city birds that cruise grassy patches for insects.

Camels have lived in Egypt for about 2,500 years. They are seen everywhere—from desert wastelands to city streets. Camels can go for days or weeks without water.

They are called "ships of the desert" because they navigate vast oceans of sand. A camel can carry a 600-pound (272-kg) load for 30 miles (48 km), and camels bred for racing can run up to 10 miles (16 km) per hour for eighteen hours.

Egypt's camels are dromedaries, or one-humped camels. They store fat, not water, in their hump, but given the chance, a camel can drink 25 gallons (95 l) of water without stopping.

Ibex are wild mountain goats with long, curved horns.

An Egyptian man feeds clover to his camels near the Great Pyramids.

The Beetle That Pushed the Sun

The scarab is a beetle that crawls along pushing a huge ball of dung, or animal waste. To ancient Egyptians, the scarab represented Khepri, the god of the dawning sun. All through the night, Khepri pushed the sun across the darkness so that it could rise the next day. Good-luck charms, jewelry, and signature seals were made in the shape of scarabs. Scarabs are still pushing their dung balls around Egypt today.

The Cat—Not Just a Pet

Wild cats were first domesticated, or tamed as pets, in Egypt. The cat was a sacred animal in ancient Egypt. It was thought to represent the goddess Bastet, daughter of the sun god Re. Bronze statues of cats filled Bastet's temple near Zagazig. Cats were mummified and buried in special cat cemeteries. Hundreds of thousands of cats were recently found in a cemetery in Thebes. Today, wild cats and swamp cats slink around in the Delta.

Pigeon Houses

Scattered around Egypt's countryside are tall, rounded, earthen towers full of holes. These strange structures are pigeon houses. The villagers know that pigeons always return to nest in the place where they hatched. When a pigeon house's holes are filled with nesting birds, villagers are assured of a steady supply of tasty pigeon meat, year after year. Also, the pigeon droppings make good fertilizer for crops.

Camels have a bad reputation for spitting, kicking, and biting, but their gentle, lurching pace is a first-class comfort on long trips. The word "camel" may come from *jamil*, an Arabic word meaning "beauty" or from *jamala*, "to bear."

Life in the Coral Reefs

Coral reefs line the underwater banks of the Red Sea. A coral reef is actually made of skeletons. Tiny animals called coral polyps live in huge colonies along the coast. When the polyps die, new polyps attach themselves to the skeletons. Generation after generation, millions of skeletons build up to form a massive reef.

A school of sweepers in the Red Sea's colorful coral reefs

The coral reef is home to a rainbow of colorful sea creatures—red sponges, pink organ-pipe sponges, and green sea anemones, as well as prickly sea urchins and feathery fanworms. In and out of this maze swim blue tangs, red groupers, angelfish, butterfly fish, parrot fish, blue-and-white Napoleon fish, lionfish, surgeonfish, sharks, and moray eels. Inching along the bottom are sea slugs and giant clams.

Ras Muhammad National Park

Ras Muhammad National Park, on the Sinai's southern tip, protects wild animals and plants on land and in the water. Its mangrove forests are the most northerly specimens in the world. Foxes and gazelles roam the park, and dozens of bird species nest there. Divers can see manta rays, reef sharks, and 6-foot (1.8-m) Napoleon fish.

A pink Egyptian lotus

The papyrus and the lotus were political symbols in ancient Egypt. As early as 3500 B.C., Egyptians used fibers of the papyrus plant to make writing paper. The plant became so important to their culture that it was used as a *hieroglyph*, or writing symbol, to represent the Delta, or kingdom of Lower Egypt. Today, papyrus is cultivated mainly in the Delta region and rarely grows in the wild.

The lotus, a flowering aquatic plant that once grew all along the Nile, was the royal symbol for Upper Egypt. Today, it is found only in the Delta, in hidden bends of the Nile, and in the Fayyum.

Tall reeds thrive along the Nile's banks and on its islands. Acacias brighten the riverbanks with their yellow flowers. The water hyacinth, however, is a beautiful, blue-flowered pest. This hardy plant spreads fast and clogs irrigation canals.

The tamarisk shrubs that grow around Lake Nasser and the Sinai ooze a sweet, sticky substance that herdsmen sell to tourists. It is believed to be the manna the Israelites ate in the desert in Biblical times.

Date palms grow along the Nile and in the oases along with groves of citrus, pomegranate, and apricot trees. A sharp, aromatic smell is a sign that eucalyptus trees are nearby. Egypt's only forests are the mangrove forests on the coasts of the Red Sea and the southeast Sinai. The roots of saltwater mangrove trees grow partly under water and partly above the surface.

The beautiful water hyacinth grows quickly and obstructs canals.

A date picker uses a rope to climb a date palm.

Land of the Pharaohs

People were farming along the Nile as early as 7000 B.C. Eventually, they settled into two kingdoms—Upper Egypt in the south, and Lower Egypt in the northern Delta. In about 3100 B.C., Menes, a king of Upper Egypt, united the two kingdoms. Menes was honored as Egypt's first pharaoh, or king. (The word *pharaoh* comes from the words *per 'aa*, meaning "big house.")

PHARAOHS LIKED TO KEEP THEIR power in the family. Ancient Egypt was governed by one dynasty, or ruling family, after another. Thirty-one dynasties of pharaohs reigned in Egypt between 3100 B.C. and 332 B.C.

Levels of Society

The pharaoh and his family were at the top rung of Egyptian society. They lived in great luxury. Alabaster lamps, golden beds and chairs, and exotic woods inlaid with ivory decorated their homes. Servants took care of their every need. Musicians and dancers amused guests at their lavish banquets. Other members of the upper class were priests, nobles, doctors, and high-ranking army officers.

Artisans, merchants, and engineers made up the middle class. Scribes, or professional writers, held a special place of honor. Every family hoped to have a son who would become a scribe. The scribes wrote letters and government documents and recorded the pharaohs' decrees.

Ancient Egyptian society greatly valued scribes. This painted limestone sculpture is on display at the Louvre Museum in Paris.

The common people were farmers, laborers, and soldiers. Farming took only part of the year so many farmers spent several months working on the pharaohs' construction projects.

Love and Marriage

In ancient Egypt, love was an important part of marriage. Egyptians wrote beautiful love poems and songs. Druggists mixed love potions to help people charm their beloved. Pharaohs could keep several wives, but one wife was customary for everyone else.

Women in ancient Egypt had more rights than women in many cultures have today. They could own property, buy and sell goods, and inherit wealth. Wives could even sue for divorce if they had a good reason.

Homes, Adornments, and Games

Most people lived in simple houses made of mud bricks. Very few of these houses remain today. Centuries of rain and wind have swept the soft materials away. In these simple homes, people sat and slept on woven mats on the floor. Candles and oil lamps provided light at night. Wealthy people had beautiful homes with dozens of rooms. Some were built around courtyards with gardens and pools.

Women kept their makeup in tiny bowls and jars. Cosmetics were made from minerals and plants. Gypsum was mixed with soot to make a sparkly eye shadow. A black substance called *kohl* was used as an eyeliner. Other substances made red coloring for lips and blush for cheeks. Women also painted their fingernails and wore hair ornaments. Upper-class women wore earrings, bracelets, armbands, and necklaces of gold and precious stones.

Both men and women wore light-weight linen skirts or robes. Lower-class people went barefoot, while the upper classes wore leather sandals. Shoulder-length head coverings protected workers from the heat of the sun. Upper-class men and women wore wigs. On festive evenings, women sometimes wore a cone of perfumed animal fat on their heads. As the night wore on, the fat melted, drenching them with sweet-smelling oil.

Ancient paintings and artifacts show how much the Egyptians loved games. Children played leapfrog and tug-of-war. Girls played catch with a ball, sometimes while riding piggyback. Wooden toys included monkeys on horseback and animals on wheels. Grown-ups played a game called *senet* by moving pieces on a checkered board. They played "snake" on a round board shaped like a coiled snake.

Nefertiti, queen of Egypt during 1300s B.C., was noted for her beauty.

Ancient Cuisine

Egyptians ate using the first three fingers of the right hand. A typical meal might include vegetables such as broad beans, lentils, peas, cucumbers, or cabbage. People also enjoyed onions, garlic, turnips, and lettuce. Their fruit trees yielded figs, dates, and pomegranates. Other favorite fruits were melons and grapes.

Hunters went into the desert for wild game such as antelope and gazelle. In marshy areas, they shot ducks and geese with bows and arrows. Quail, pigeon, and beef were grilled or roasted. Fish from the Nile were salted or hung out to dry. Food was sweetened with honey collected from beehives.

Bread was a basic, everyday food. Pharaohs and nobles had their own bakeries. In most homes, women ground wheat and barley into flour and baked the loaves in clay pots or beehive-shaped clay ovens.

Beer and ale were popular drinks, even for children. They were produced in breweries by fermenting barley or wheat. Wine was made from grapes and dates. It was preserved and labeled in sealed bottles.

A hunting relief from the temple of Ramses II

The Cycle of Floods

Ancient Egyptians divided the year into three seasons of four months each. The new year began with the flooding of the Nile in July. This was the season of *akhet*. In November, as the waters receded, *peret*—the plowing and planting season—began. The dry season, *shemu*, lasted from March to July. Then crops were harvested and stored before the rains came again.

This detail from a tomb wall in Thebes shows men trampling grapes to make wine.

Ancient Egyptians used nilometers to measure the Nile's water level. This nilometer is in Cairo.

Opposite: **Hieroglyphs cover this obelisk at Luxor Temple.**

The floodwaters left a deposit of silt that fertilized the fields and produced abundant crops. Mud along the riverbank was made into pots, jars, tiles, and other ceramics. People measured the rise and fall of the Nile's water level with a *nilometer*—a series of marks on riverside rocks or cliffs.

Farmers produced more than enough food for Egypt's people. The pharaohs' storehouses brimmed over with the food they collected as taxes. Ancient Egypt has been called the "granary [grainhouse] to the world." Grain and other crops were traded with neighboring peoples in Africa and Asia.

Animal Life

Ancient Egypt swarmed with animals that no longer live there. Hippopotamuses bobbed in the Nile and lounged along the shore. Lions wandered in from the desert for water. Baboons and wildcats screeched in the thickets, and herds of gazelles trotted by. Golden jackals scoured the valleys for animal and human remains. Great flocks of rose-colored flamingos swooped in to nest along the Nile, and red-breasted geese flew in to winter in the marshes.

As the climate grew hotter and dryer, human settlements spread, and these animals went away. We know they once lived there because Egyptians left paintings of them. Ancient animals that still live in Egypt include cobras, crocodiles, vultures, falcons, quails, and cows. Many animals were drawn in hieroglyphic symbols, and some were honored as gods.

Hieroglyphs

Egyptians were writing with picture symbols called hieroglyphs as early as 3000 B.C. Some hieroglyphs represented an object. For example, wavy lines stood for water, and a bird was—a bird. But a picture could also stand for an idea. Walking feet meant movement or the passage of time.

Some hieroglyphic symbols were homophones—words that sound alike but have different meanings. For example, the pharaoh Narmer's name was written as *n'r* (fish) plus *mr* (chisel). (Vowel sounds were often left out.) Some symbols stood for sounds. Others showed whether a word was singular or plural or a noun or a verb. By 300 B.C., the

U	B	P	F	M	N
W	KH	S	S	A E	Y
O	TH	N	R	L	H
SH	K or C	Q	G	T	D
C H	M	U	O	MAN	ANKH
WOMAN	MEN	H	A	DJ	I

Chart of hieroglyphic symbols

Egyptian alphabet consisted of more than 700 hieroglyphic symbols.

A loop with a royal name inside it was called a *cartouche*. You can make your own cartouche using the symbols shown in the hieroglyphic chart.

Gods and Goddesses

Ancient Egyptians worshiped many gods and goddesses. They believed their gods caused the sun to rise, the Nile to flood, the crops to grow, and the cows to give milk. Each town and family had its own special gods. The pharaoh himself was seen as a god who protected the people.

Priests took care of the temples and made offerings at the proper times. Re, the sun god, was the most important of all the gods. Amon, the sun god of Thebes, was combined with Re as Amon-Re. His temple at Karnak, near Luxor, was a great center of worship

Major Gods and Goddesses of Ancient Egypt

Horus
Mythical first pharaoh.
Sky god associated with
Re. Son of Isis and Osiris.
Often shown as a hawk
or falcon.

Amon—Supreme deity of Thebes. Wears a headdress with two tall plumes.

Aton—Represented the sun at its highest point in the sky.

Hathor—Daughter of Re and Nut, goddess of joy, love, and music. Shown with cow's head.

Isis—Great mother-goddess. Sister/wife of Osiris. Protected children and taught women the arts of home-making. Sometimes shown with a throne on her head.

Anubis
Led the dead into the
afterworld. Pictured with
jackal's head.

Re
Sun god. Pictured as a falcon, scarab,
or sun disk. Honored at Heliopolis.

Nut—Mother of Osiris. Covered the skies, swallowing the sun every night and giving birth to it again every morning.

Osiris—God of corn and fertile crops. Husband/brother of Isis. Shown as a mummy holding a king's staff and whip.

Ptah—Chief god of Memphis. Patron of artists and crafts-people. Pictured with a close-fitting gown and cap.

Thoth—God of wisdom, who invented hieroglyphics. Shown with the head of an ibis.

Temple of Amon at Karnak

for hundreds of years. One pharaoh after another built additions onto the temple until it covered a huge area.

Life Everlasting

The age of 110 was believed to be the perfect life span, but it was more an ideal than a reality. Most people in those days did not live past their thirties. But every Egyptian, from pharaoh to laborer, believed in life after death. Given the proper burial rites, they could be immortal.

The Egyptians believed that the jackal-headed god Anubis escorted each soul into the afterlife. Osiris, god of the underworld, made a final judgment by the "weighing of the heart." A feather was put on one side of a scale, and the person's heart on the other side. If the heart was as light as the feather, the soul could enter eternity.

Egyptians also believed that the dead would enjoy all their earthly comforts in the afterlife. Burial chambers were filled with favorite possessions, clothes, furniture, games, and food. Even pet cats were preserved and buried with their masters.

Mummies

After death, the body was made into a mummy to keep it from decaying. This ensured a successful journey into the after-life. Mummification could take as long as seventy days.

First, the body was packed in a salt called natron, which dried the tissues and kept them from breaking down. Then the internal organs were removed. Some were preserved in jars and buried with the body. Other organs were treated with herbs and replaced in the body. The brain, believed to be worth-less, was thrown away. Em-balming fluids and pastes were then applied to preserve the skin and the body's interior.

Finally, the body was wrapped round and round with white linen strips. Mummies of some pharaohs were encased in jewel-encrusted gold and placed in a sarcophagus, or stone coffin, in the burial chamber. Scrolls of the *Book of the Dead* were buried with the body. They contained special prayers and

A mummified body

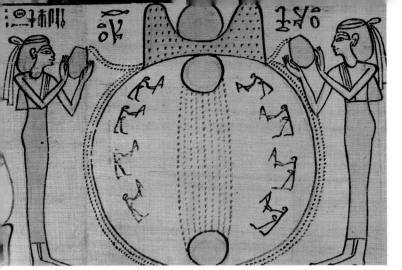

A papyrus scroll from the *Book of the Dead*

instructions for getting through the mysterious world of the dead.

Pyramids

To make sure they would have eternal life, pharaohs built fabulous tombs for themselves. The earliest pharaohs built tombs called *mastabas*—low, flat-topped, mud-brick structures with slanting sides.

Djoser, a pharaoh of the Third Dynasty, wanted a more glorious tomb, so his architect, Imhotep, built the first pyramid. It is called a step pyramid because its sides are like stair steps. Djoser's step pyramid still stands at Saqqara, near Memphis.

Fourth Dynasty pharaohs built the most famous pyramids—the three pyramids of Giza, just west of Cairo. Khufu built the largest one, called the Great Pyramid, around 2600 B.C. Khufu's pyramid was made of limestone blocks covered with sheer granite slabs that glistened in the sun. People could slide right down the sides. In later centuries, the granite was removed to make buildings in Cairo.

Khufu's son Khafre and the pharaoh Menkaure built the two other Giza pyramids. Nearby stands the Great Sphinx, a massive stone lion with the head of a man.

Great Pyramid Facts

Height: 481 feet (147 m)—taller than a forty-story building

Length of One Side: 755 feet (230 m), or one-seventh of a mile

Area Covered: 13 acres (5 ha), or about seven city blocks

Number of Limestone Blocks: About 2.5 million

Average Weight of a Block: 2.5 tons

Weight of Heaviest Blocks: 15 tons

Contents: Stolen by grave robbers, probably in ancient times

How Did They Build the Pyramids?

The ancient Egyptians left only a few clues about how they built the pyramids. From rock quarries at Aswan, stone blocks were floated down the Nile on rafts for 500 miles (800 km). Then the blocks were probably put on runners, like sleds, and hauled up wooden or stone ramps.

The Greek historian Herodotus says that 100,000 men worked on the Great Pyramid in three-month shifts. Then another 100,000 went to work. This went on for more than twenty years. How were the blocks lifted into place? According to Herodotus, they were lifted with a kind of crane that rested on lower-level stones.

Pharaoh Djoser's step pyramid in Saqqara—the first pyramid in ancient Egypt—was built in about 2650 B.C. Funerary temples are in the foreground.

Who Is the Sphinx? Where Is Its Nose?

The Great Sphinx's head is six stories high, and its lion's body is four-fifths as long as a football field. Its face is believed to be a portrait of Khafre, son of Khufu. But some researchers think the statue was carved long before Khafre's time. They point to the rocks' erosion pattern, which looks more like water erosion than wind erosion. That would place the Sphinx in a time when heavy rains and floods were common in Egypt—perhaps even 10,000 years ago. Regardless of its age, the Sphinx has been badly damaged by wind, sandstorms, rain, and pollution. Its nose is completely gone. Workers are now giving it a "facelift" by restoring crumbling stones.

Timeline of Dynasties

3110 B.C.	Founding of united Egypt by King Menes
c. 2686 B.C.–2160 B.C.	Old Kingdom
c. 2040 B.C.–1786 B.C.	Middle Kingdom
1570 B.C.–330 B.C.	New Kingdom

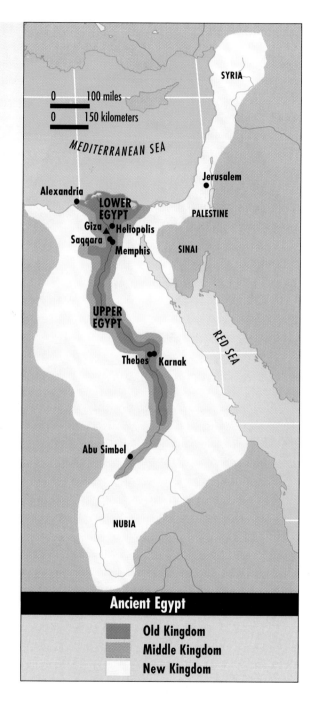

Ancient Egypt

- Old Kingdom
- Middle Kingdom
- New Kingdom

Kingdoms Unite and Divide

The history of ancient Egypt may be divided into three major periods—the Old Kingdom, the Middle Kingdom, and the New Kingdom. Memphis was Egypt's capital during the Old Kingdom period, beginning around 2686 B.C. Memphis lies about 15 miles (24 km) south of what is now Cairo. Even in this early period, Egyptians were making paper from papyrus fibers and writing in hieroglyphs.

In time, the pharaohs' power weakened, and Egypt once again broke into separate districts. Mentuhotep II pulled the kingdom together again around 2040 B.C. He built his capital at Thebes, on the Nile's east bank in Upper Egypt. His reign marks the beginning of the Middle

Statue of Thutmose III

Kingdom period. During this time, construction began on the temple of Amon at Karnak.

Asian people called the Hyksos rose to power in the 1600s B.C. They began ruling from their capital at Avaris in the Delta and later spread to Thebes. Egyptians learned much about the art of war from these foreign rulers. The Hyksos introduced horse-drawn chariots, bronze and iron swords, and other military gear.

The New Kingdom: Conquests and Construction

Ahmose, a Theban prince, drove the Hyksos out in the 1500s B.C. This began the New Kingdom period, with Thebes as the capital. With their new military skills, Egyptians now became a major world power. Under Thutmose III, they took over Nubia, Palestine, Syria, and northern Iraq. New lands meant new sources of wealth. Slaves, exotic woods, ivory, and precious metals and stones poured into the pharaohs' warehouses.

To show off their power, New Kingdom pharaohs built huge temples, monuments, and statues of themselves.

Ramses II ("Ramses the Great") was the greatest builder of all. He built the temples at Abu Simbel and enlarged the temple at Karnak. Scholars also believe he was the pharaoh mentioned in the Bible's Book of Exodus story, in which Moses led the Hebrews out of slavery in Egypt.

For their tombs, New Kingdom rulers built huge necropolises, or cities of the dead. These tomb sites were on the west bank of the Nile, across from Thebes. Today they are named the Valley of the Kings, the Valley of the Queens, and the Tombs of the Nobles.

In 1995, archaeologist Kent Weeks discovered what may be the largest tomb in the Valley of the Kings. It holds most of Ramses II's fifty-two sons. So far, about sixty tombs have been found in the Valley of the Kings—only a fraction of those waiting to be discovered.

Hatshepsut, the Female Pharaoh

Hatshepsut was the daughter of Thutmose I and the wife of Thutmose II. When her husband died, his son and successor, Thutmose III, was still a child. Hatshepsut was expected to rule in the boy's place until he grew up, but she wanted more. She had herself crowned as the pharaoh and ruled for twenty-two years. In art, Hatshepsut is sometimes shown dressed as a male pharaoh. For her tomb, she built a magnificent temple at Deir al-Bahri near the Valley of the Kings. It was completely hewn from a solid stone mountainside.

The temple of Ramses II at Abu Simbel features four immense statues of the pharaoh.

The Boy King

We know about Tutankhamen, or "King Tut," from his lavish tomb in the Valley of the Kings. Tutankhamen, the "boy king," reigned in the 1300s B.C. He died when he was about eighteen years old. More than 5,000 objects were found in his tomb, including furniture, games, weapons, and a golden chariot. Among the clothes in his tomb were 28 pairs of gloves, 25 head coverings, and 145 loincloths.

Ramses III of the Twentieth Dynasty was the last great New Kingdom pharaoh. In later dynasties, foreigners from Nubia, Libya, Ethiopia, and Assyria held the throne. Cambyses, the son of Persia's Cyrus the Great, invaded Egypt in 525 B.C., and Persian pharaohs ruled for the next 200 years.

Alexander and the Ptolemies

In 332 B.C., Alexander the Great marched into Egypt. Just twenty-four years old, he already ruled the Greek empire. Now he was hacking away at the Persian empire. Egyptians were glad to have Alexander deliver them from the Persians. In Memphis, he was enthroned as pharaoh. He built his capital city on the Mediterranean coast and named it Alexandria. Alexander also paid a visit to the famous oracle, or fortune-teller, at Siwa. Rumors said the oracle declared Alexander a god.

Before he died in 323 B.C., Alexander divided his empire among his finest generals. Egypt went to Ptolemy, who installed himself as pharaoh. The Ptolemies reigned for the next 300 years.

During the Ptolemaic period, Egypt was drenched in Greek culture. Greek scholars and scientists made Alexandria the cultural capital of the Mediterranean. Astronomers, mathematicians, doctors, and engineers worked and studied there. Alexandria's library and museum had the most magnificent collection of manuscripts and documents in the world.

Across the Mediterranean from Egypt, another great empire was on the rise. The Roman Empire was spreading

across southern Europe and into Asia. Naturally, the Romans turned their eyes to Egypt. For years, the Ptolemies paid exorbitant taxes to Rome. Cleopatra, the last Ptolemy ruler, paid, too. But she had a plan.

In 1995, archaeologist Kent Weeks discovered a tomb containing most of Ramses II's fifty-two sons.

Lighthouse to Ancient Mariners

In 1995, archaeologist Jean-Yves Empereur dredged up massive chunks of granite from the murky waters of Alexandria Bay. They turned out to be pieces of the world's first lighthouse, the legendary Pharos of Alexandria.

Built in the third century B.C., the Pharos was called one of the Seven Wonders of the Ancient World. It stood over 400 feet (122 m) high in Alexandria's harbor. A fire burned continuously from its peak, while a mirror reflected the light to ships as far as 70 miles (113 km) away.

An earthquake reduced the lighthouse to rubble in 1375. For over 600 years, the Pharos remained only a mysterious legend. "At last we can put our finger on the myth," said Empereur.

Cleopatra and Mark Antony

Queen Cleopatra, shown here receiving Mark Antony, was the last of the Ptolemaic rulers. She died in 30 B.C.

Cleopatra knew that Egypt was in grave danger. She also knew that Rome had become the greatest military power in the world and, she believed, her best chance to save her kingdom was to join forces with Rome. She befriended Julius Caesar, the Roman emperor, and they had a son. After Caesar was assassinated, she married one of his generals, Mark Antony. The marriage suited Mark Antony's ambitions, too. With his forces and Egypt's combined, he could defeat his rival, Octavian, and rule the whole Roman Empire.

Unfortunately for the wedded couple, things did not work out as they had planned. Octavian conquered Egypt's forces at the sea battle of Actium in 31 B.C., and he captured Alexandria the following year. Seeing that they had lost everything, Mark Antony and Cleopatra committed suicide, and Egypt became a Roman province. The days of the pharaohs were over.

CHAPTER

FIVE

The Long Road to Freedom

Life was rough for Egyptians under Roman rule. The Roman governors demanded huge taxes and forced Egyptian peasants to serve in the Roman army. Loads of grain from Egypt's farms were shipped to Rome.

In the first century a.d., Christianity sprang up in the Roman Empire. In Egypt, the Christian community was known as the Coptic Church. Seeing the new religion as a threat, Roman emperors outlawed it and began executing Christians. In the third century, Emperor Diocletian had thousands of Egypt's Christians put to death. Later emperors reversed the rule. In a.d. 313, Emperor Constantine converted to Christianity, and later Theodosius made it the Roman Empire's official religion.

In a.d. 395, the Roman Empire split in two. Rome was the capital of the Western Empire, and the Eastern, or Byzantine, Empire was ruled from Constantinople (now Istanbul, Turkey). Egypt became part of the Byzantine Empire. As the Byzantines weakened, Egypt became ripe for another takeover.

A Byzantine mosaic from Saint Catherine's Monastery

The Arab Invasion

Across the Red Sea in Arabia, Muhammad was preaching the new religion of Islam. Muhammad's teachings spread like wildfire. His followers, called Muslims, waged holy wars across Arabia and north into Syria and Persia. In 639, the Arab army under Amr ibn al-As invaded Egypt, taking Cairo in 641 and Alexandria in 642. Amr ibn al-As built the walled military city of *Fustat* (Old Cairo) in 643.

Gradually, Arabic ways mixed with local customs or replaced them altogether. The native Coptic language gave way to Arabic as Egypt's official tongue. Islam became the official religion, and the ancient cultures of the pharaohs, Persians, Greeks, and Romans all but disappeared.

The First Caliphs

After Muhammad's death, military and religious leaders called caliphs ruled Islamic lands. They set up powerful dynasties. Each dynasty claimed to be descended from Muhammad, and each practiced Islam in its own way. Armed with their beliefs, they fought each other for control of Muslim territory.

At first, Egypt became a province under the Umayyad caliphs. The Umayyads claimed to be descended from Umayya, a cousin of Muhammad's grandfather. Their capital was Damascus, in Syria.

Abbasid caliphs took over Egypt in 750. They ruled their empire from Baghdad, in present-day Iraq. The Abbasids followed the Sunni form of Islam, claiming authority through Abbas, Muhammad's uncle. Abbasids had powerful armies, but they could not defend Egypt from its own neighbors.

Who's in Charge?

bey—a local governor

caliph—the head ruler in a Muslim dynasty

emir—a regional Muslim ruler

imam—a descendant of Muhammad through his son-in-law Ali

khedive—a representative of the Ottoman sultan

sultan—prince of a territory within a dynasty

The Fatimids

The Fatimid dynasty ruled Tunisia, a North African land west of Egypt. Fatimids were Shiite Muslims, who considered Muhammad's son-in-law Ali to be his spiritual heir. Jawhar, a great Fatimid general, occupied Egypt in 969. Caliph al-Muizz built al-Qahirah (Cairo) in 973 and made it his capital. From there, he overpowered Arabia, Palestine, and Syria.

Egypt prospered under the Fatimids. Merchant ships from India and China brought goods to Alexandria and the Red Sea ports. Egypt then traded these goods with cities in Italy. Al-Azhar University was founded for Shiite Islamic studies. Arts and literature flourished, and Cairo became a center of learning.

As Islam spread, the Christian Church watched its holy lands being taken over. Pope Urban II, as head of the Church, called upon Christians everywhere to fight Crusades, or holy wars, and regain Christian lands. Crusaders focused on Jerusalem, in Palestine, and other places they regarded as holy. In the 1100s, Crusaders marched against the Fatimids in Egypt, paving the way for the Fatimids to fall to Saladin.

Saladin and the Ayyubids

Saladin is one of the most famous warriors in history. His Arabic name, *Salah ad-Din*, means "the bounty of religion."

As a young man, Saladin studied religion in Damascus. When the Fatimids asked Syria for help against the Crusaders, he joined his uncle's army in Egypt. To Saladin and most Egyptians, the Abbasids were Egypt's rightful rulers. When the

Fatimid caliph al-Adid died in 1171, Saladin took over. When Syria's sultan died in 1174, Saladin annexed Syria, too.

As sultan of Egypt and Syria, Saladin established the Ayyubid dynasty. He changed the teachings at al-Azhar University to the Sunni form of Islam. Saladin's greatest goal still lay ahead—to drive the Crusaders out of Palestine and reunite Muslim lands. He went on to capture Jerusalem in 1187 and drove the Crusaders to a few coastal towns.

The Mamelukes

Ayyubid rulers surrounded themselves with a bevy of soldier-bodyguards called Mamelukes—slaves from Turkey, Greece, and central Asia. Mamelukes were taken as boys and trained to be soldiers and government officials. Once their training was over, they were free. Some held high positions and became very powerful.

In 1250, the Mamelukes took control of Egypt. Their greatest leader was Baybars, a general who became the fourth Mameluke sultan. Baybars drove Mongol invaders out of Palestine, took over Syria, and won many towns away from the Crusaders.

Saladin, the great Muslim leader, fought against the Crusaders.

Mameluke merchants carried on trade with Europe and Asia. With their vast wealth, they supported beautiful architecture and fine ceramics and metalwork. In time, however, the Mameluke army split into rival groups and lost its fighting edge.

Ottoman Rule

Selim, a sultan of the Turkish Ottoman Empire, knew his well-equipped army had an unbeatable weapon—newly invented cannons. Selim seized Syria in 1516 and captured

In 1798, the Mamelukes submitted to Napoleon Bonaparte.

Cairo in 1517, installing himself as caliph. In time, much of the Arab world looked to Selim as its leader and protector.

Egypt remained a province of the Ottoman Empire for almost 300 years. While Ottoman caliphs ruled in Cairo, Mamelukes served as beys, or local administrators. These officials lived apart from the Egyptian peasants. Some beys kept order and collected taxes, but many were simply the elite, with no particular duties.

Napoleon and the French

Napoleon Bonaparte of France sailed a fleet of ships to Egypt's coast on July 1, 1798. In the Battle of the Pyramids near Cairo, Napoleon conquered the Mameluke army and took control of Egypt. He organized a modern government, started irrigation projects, and planned a Suez canal route. French scholars and scientists studied Egypt's culture and farming practices. Archaeologists began to uncover ancient Egypt's buried treasures.

In 1799, Napoleon returned to France, leaving his generals to keep order. Now Great Britain saw its chance to get a foothold in Egypt. British troops joined forces with the Ottomans and Mamelukes. Together, they hammered away at the French until they pulled out in 1801.

Muhammad Ali and His Successors

Muhammad Ali, Egypt's Ottoman governor, had learned a lot from watching the British and French. He realized that Europe was far ahead of Egypt in many ways. When he took

Champollion and the Rosetta Stone

In 1799, near the Egyptian town of Rosetta, a French officer discovered a slab of stone inscribed with three sets of strange writing. One was hieroglyphic symbols, but no one knew how to read them. The slab (right), named the Rosetta Stone, went to a museum. Jean-François Champollion (left) cracked the mystery in 1822. Two of the inscriptions were in languages that he knew—Greek and demotic, a later form of Egyptian writing. To his surprise, the inscriptions said the same thing. By comparing the hieroglyphs to the other two writings, he developed a hieroglyphic "dictionary."

office in 1805, he set to work modernizing the country. He brought in French military advisers to train his army. Factories were built to make textiles and process iron. Schools of medicine and engineering were opened, and European scholars came to lecture. Bright young Egyptians studied in Europe, then came back and translated their textbooks into Arabic.

Muhammad Ali's son, Said Pasha, ruled Egypt from 1854 to 1863. He granted a French company the right to build a canal from the Mediterranean to the Gulf of Suez. The Suez Canal opened to traffic in 1869.

Said's nephew, Ismail, improved Egypt's schools, roads, railroads, and factories. But his lavish spending on palaces and other luxuries cast Egypt deep into debt. In 1875, to raise money, Ismail sold Egypt's shares in the Suez Canal to Great Britain, making France and Britain the canal's primary owners.

British Rule

Fed up with foreigners, Egyptians revolted in 1882. But British forces subdued the rebels and occupied the country. When World War I (1914–1918) broke out, the British declared Egypt a protectorate. This implied that the British were protecting Egypt, but actually they were protecting the Suez Canal.

In 1922, the British granted independence to Egypt but continued to run much of the country's affairs. The British

The Curse of King Tut

Rumors said that an ancient curse guarded King Tut's tomb. After November 4, 1922, when British archaeologist Howard Carter discovered the fabulous tomb of King Tutankhamen, a cholera epidemic broke out in Luxor. Then more than a dozen of Carter's friends died mysteriously after visiting the tomb. Meanwhile, Carter's partner, Lord Carnarvon, was bitten by a mosquito as he left the site. The bite led to blood poisoning, and he died. Back in England, at the very moment of Carnarvon's death, his dog Susie howled madly and fell dead. Some say that the "curse" rumor was started by a newspaperman who was jealous that Carter had sold his story to a rival newspaper. Others say the deaths were caused by bacteria from the tomb.

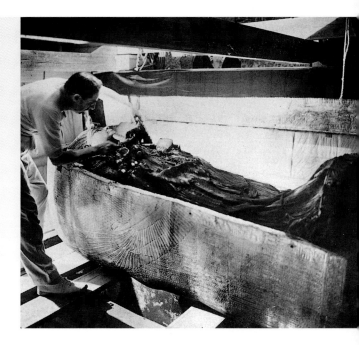

German leader Erwin Rommel in Egypt

German soldiers march through the desert in the Battle of el-Alamein.

army stayed for World War II (1939–1945)—again, to protect the canal. In 1942, Germany's Field Marshal Erwin Rommel, the "Desert Fox," landed German and Italian forces on Egypt's Mediterranean coast. At the two-week-long Battle of el-Alamein, British general Bernard Montgomery forced Rommel into retreat.

After the war, the United Nations divided Palestine to make a homeland for Jewish people. Egypt and other Arab countries protested, but the Jewish state of Israel became a reality in 1948. Conflict between Israel and the Arab states continues to this day.

Nasser and the Revolution

After centuries of outside rule, Egyptians were ready to take control of their own country. On July 23, 1952, army officers led by Lieutenant Colonel Gamal Abdel Nasser overthrew King Farouk's regime. Egypt was declared a republic in 1953, and Nasser became prime minister the next year. In 1956, he won the presidency.

President Nasser tried to solve many of the problems that troubled his country. He urged rural people to stay in their villages and affirm their Egyptian identity. New laws gave more peasants a chance to own land. Public schools were improved, and graduates were given government jobs. One of the major events of Nasser's rule was the Suez Canal crisis.

Gamal Abdel Nasser

Gamal Abdel Nasser (1918–1970), president of Egypt from 1956 to 1970, is considered the father of modern Egypt. He led the revolution of 1952, after which Egypt became a republic.

The Canal Crisis and the Six-Day War

Nasser planned to build the Aswan High Dam, but he needed money to do it. The United States, Britain, and the World Bank at first agreed to lend the money. Later, they withdrew the offer. In 1956, Nasser responded by taking control of the Suez Canal—a move that made him a hero in the Arab world. Nasser then took over Egypt's banks and private industries. Nearly 250,000 foreigners were required to leave the country.

In 1958, Syria and Egypt formed the United Arab Republic (UAR), with Nasser as president. Yemen (Sana), on the

During the Suez Canal crisis in 1956, Egyptians sank their own vessels in the canal to block British and French warships.

Anwar Sadat

Anwar Sadat (1918–1981) was Egypt's president from 1970 to 1981. He shared the 1978 Nobel Peace Prize with Israeli prime minister Menachem Begin. The two signed the 1978 Camp David Accords and the 1979 Egypt-Israel peace treaty.

Arabian Peninsula, joined the UAR too. This union lasted only three years, but Egypt kept the name United Arab Republic.

Meanwhile, Israelis and Palestinian Arabs were in constant conflict. In June 1967, Egypt closed the Gulf of Aqaba to Israeli ships. Israel then stormed into several Arab countries, including Egypt, and occupied the Sinai in the Six-Day War.

Israel's victory humiliated Egypt and other Arab states. Islamic fundamentalists began to call for a return to strict Islam as the only way to achieve victory over Israel.

Sadat and Middle East Peace

After President Nasser's death in 1970, Anwar Sadat became president. In 1971, Sadat changed Egypt's official name to the

Arab Republic of Egypt. He reopened Egypt's doors to foreign businesses to help the economy, but Sadat's main concern was Israel.

In October 1973, Sadat sent troops across the Suez Canal in an effort to win back the Israeli-occupied lands. In eighteen days of fighting, called the October War, not much was accomplished. Hoping to make peace, Sadat visited Israeli prime minister Menachem Begin in 1977. The following year, Sadat and Begin met in the United States and signed the Camp David Accords. The long-time enemies signed a peace treaty, and Sinai was restored to Egypt.

In October 1981, Sadat was shot dead as he stood on a public platform. The assassins were members of *al-Jihad*, a

Muhammad Hosni Mubarak

Muhammad Hosni Mubarak (1928–) became president of Egypt after the assassination of Anwar Sadat in 1981. Before that, he served as Egypt's vice president (1975–1981), air force commander (1972–1975), and air force chief of staff (1969–1972).

Muslim fundamentalist group. Vice President Hosni Mubarak then became president.

Challenges, Old and New

Like Sadat, President Mubarak chose a path of tolerance and moderation. At home, his most difficult task has been combating terrorism. On the bright side, his economic reforms are making Egypt stronger and wealthier.

Egypt faces threats to peace on almost every side. Militant governments rule Libya and Algeria to the west and Sudan to the south. To the northeast, problems with Israel, Iraq, and Iran continue. President Mubarak's efforts to keep peace in the Middle East earn the gratitude of the world community.

The Arab Republic

The Arab Republic of Egypt (*Misr* in Arabic) adopted its present constitution in 1971. It calls Egypt a socialist democratic country and part of the larger Arab nation.

Like the United States and Canada, Egypt has three branches of government. The president heads the executive branch. The People's Assembly is the legislative, or lawmaking, branch. Egypt's court system makes up the judicial branch.

I N EGYPT, THE PRESIDENT PLAYS A VERY STRONG ROLE IN THE national government. The president, as the chief executive and head of state, sets government policies and commands the armed forces.

An Egyptian president must be born of Egyptian parents and be at least forty years old. To select a president, at least one-third of the People's Assembly must nominate a candidate, and two-thirds of the members must vote their support. Next, the people approve the candidate in a referendum. The president's six-year term can be renewed. President Hosni Mubarak, elected in 1981, began a second term in 1987 and a third term in 1993.

President Hosni Mubarak (center) heads the executive branch of government.

The president appoints one or more vice presidents, a prime minister, and a council of ministers. Ministers must be at least thirty-five years old. The president also chooses many local officials.

The People's Assembly and the Shura Council

The People's Assembly, or *Majlis ash-Sha'ab*, is Egypt's lawmaking body. At least half the assembly members must come from the laborer and farmer classes. Of its 454 deputies, 444 are elected by popular vote. Two deputies come from each of 222 districts and the president nominates the

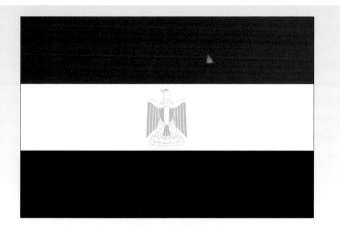

The National Flag

Egypt's flag features three horizontal bands—red, white, and black. In the center of the white band is the crest of Saladin, the national emblem. It is a golden hawk and shield with a scroll underneath. Red, white, and black are traditional colors for Arabic people. The black band represents Egypt's history before it became a republic; white stands for Egypt's peaceful revolution in 1952; and red stands for the passionate spirit of its people.

Chart of Egypt's national government

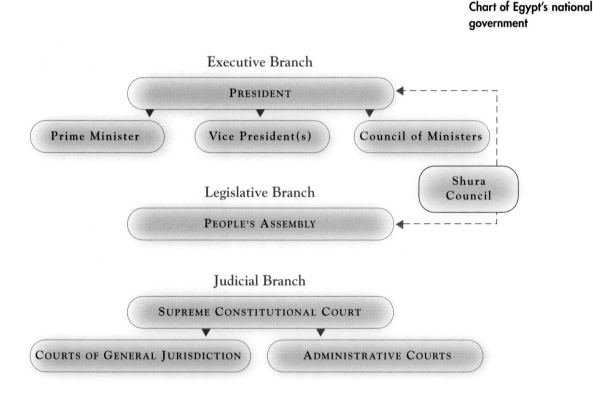

Executive Branch

PRESIDENT

Prime Minister   Vice President(s)   Council of Ministers

Shura Council

Legislative Branch

PEOPLE'S ASSEMBLY

Judicial Branch

SUPREME CONSTITUTIONAL COURT

COURTS OF GENERAL JURISDICTION   ADMINISTRATIVE COURTS

The Arab Republic   **69**

other ten. The entire People's Assembly is elected at one time, and its members serve a five-year term.

The 264-member Shura Council, or Consultative Assembly, studies national issues and drafts proposals and laws. It advises the president and the People's Assembly, although it has no lawmaking power. The president appoints one-third of its members, and voters elect the others. Shura Council members serve six-year terms.

The Courts

Egypt's judicial branch is modeled after the French court system. The Supreme Constitutional Court is Egypt's highest court. Its judges review the laws to make sure they are in line with the constitution. They also resolve conflicts between lower courts. When two courts make opposite decisions, the Supreme Court makes a ruling.

There are two types of lower courts: courts of general jurisdiction and administrative courts. The highest

court of general jurisdiction is the court of cassation. It hears disputed cases from courts of appeal. Below the courts of appeal are tribunals of first instance and district courts. Each of these is divided into civil and criminal chambers. Administrative courts handle lawsuits against the government and its agencies.

Judges decide all court cases in Egypt. There are no trials by jury.

The People's Assembly, shown here in session, is Egypt's lawmaking body. Members are elected to five-year terms.

Local Government

Egypt is divided into twenty-six governorates. The national government appoints a governor to each one. Five of the governorates are actually large cities: Cairo, Alexandria, Suez, Ismailia, and Port Said. The city of Luxor has a separate government of its own, outside the governorate system. Each governorate is divided into districts. Within the districts are towns and villages, each with a mayor and local councils.

Political Parties

To keep the peace after the revolution, political parties were outlawed in 1953. The ban was lifted in 1977, and by the mid-1990s, there were fourteen official political parties. The National Democratic Party (NDP) was founded by President Anwar Sadat in 1978, and it has dominated the government ever since.

The NDP's main rival is the Socialist Labor Party, also founded in 1978. Other parties include the Liberal Socialist Party, the National Progressive Unionist Party, the New Wafd Party, and the Muslim Brotherhood.

Strict laws control the formation of a political party. For instance, no party can be based solely on religion. That eliminates groups such as the Muslim Brotherhood. Formed in 1928, this group operates freely in Egypt, even though it is not an official party. Individual members of the Brotherhood, running as independents, have been elected to the People's Assembly.

Religion and the Government

According to Egypt's constitution, Islam is the national religion. The Islamic code of law (*Shari'a*) is the guiding principle for Egyptian law. At the same time, freedom of worship is guaranteed for people of other faiths.

Legal questions concerning marriage and family are decided by the religious law of the people involved. For most Egyptians, this is Islamic law. Christians and Jews resolve these problems within their own religious communities.

In Egypt today, the most explosive issue is the "political Islam" movement. This is a campaign to make Egypt an Islamic state governed by Islamic law. That is the aim of the Muslim Brotherhood.

The government, on the other hand, favors a more moderate path. This creates conflict in many areas of Egyptian life. Fundamentalists (strict Muslims) want Islamic law to dominate Egypt's arts, culture, education, and lifestyles. Women's clothing is one example. Fundamentalists insist that women in Egypt should wear "the veil," which covers most of the body. But the government continues to allow more liberal dress.

Freedom of the Press

In 1960, Egyptian newspapers were censored for antigovernment views. Censorship was relaxed in 1974 and ended in 1981. Egypt's constitution guarantees freedom of the press. This freedom is protected by the Supreme Press Council. Even so, most newspapers are restrained in speaking about govern-

Islam is the national religion in Egypt. Here, Muslims pray outdoors in Cairo.

ment policies. This is no surprise, since the government appoints three out of five members of each major newspaper's editorial board.

The Arab League and Middle East Peace

Under Presidents Sadat and Mubarak, Egypt has become a strong leader—and peacekeeper—in the Middle East. President Mubarak is known around the world for his wisdom

and skill in working for peace. Much of his success stems from his central role in the Arab League.

Egypt was a founding member of the Arab League in 1945. Today its members are the presidents, kings, princes, or emirs of twenty-two Arab nations. Their countries stretch across North Africa and eastward through the Arabian Peninsula.

The Arab League's headquarters are in Cairo. The league works to promote cooperation among its members in communications, culture, and trade. Peace in the Middle East is usually the biggest issue, though. Members are divided between those who want peace with Israel and those who do not.

After the Egypt-Israel peace treaty in 1979, Egypt was expelled from the league. It was readmitted in 1989. When Iraq invaded Kuwait in 1990, Egypt emerged as a leader among moderate Arab nations. It called a summit meeting of Arab leaders, demanded Iraq's withdrawal, and sent thousands

Boutros Boutros-Ghali

Dr. Boutros Boutros-Ghali (1922–) served as secretary-general of the United Nations from 1992 through 1996. He was previously Egypt's minister of foreign affairs.

of troops to help resolve hostilities. Egypt also played an important role in a 1991 Middle East peace conference in Madrid, Spain. In 1996, Mubarak brought Arab leaders together again to help resolve conflicts between Israel and Palestine.

Terrorists

Some Islamic fundamentalists in Egypt have formed violent terrorist groups such as *al-Jihad* (Holy War). A related group, *Jama'ah al-Islamiyah* (the Islamic Group), considers Sheik Omar Abdel Rahman to be its spiritual leader. He is serving a life sentence in a U.S. prison for bomb plots. Other groups include the Vanguard of Conquest and the Islamic 19.

Some terrorists aim to overthrow President Mubarak's moderate government. Others cannot tolerate Israel or any country friendly to Israel. Various groups have killed tourists and Egyptian officials, hijacked airplanes, bombed buildings, and tried to assassinate Mubarak. Even the Muslim Brotherhood condemns these terrorist attacks.

The Egyptian government has been cracking down hard on terrorism. Police are actively seeking out terrorists, and many have been jailed or executed.

Cairo

Cairo, Egypt's capital, is the largest city in Africa with a metropolitan area covering about 175 square miles (453 sq km). It sprawls across three of Egypt's governorates—Cairo, Giza, and Qalyubiya. More than 100,000 people per square mile (per 2.6 sq km) are packed into the metro area, making it one of the world's most densely populated areas.

Cairo straddles the Nile River and includes two islands—Gezira and Roda. Bridges connect the riverbanks and the

In 1996, Egyptian members of the Islamic terrorist group al-Jihad wave the Koran as they enter court in Cairo.

The capital city of Cairo, located on the Nile River, is Africa's largest city.

islands. Even on a quick tour through the Cairo area, a visitor sees monuments from 5,000 years of Egypt's history.

The most modern sections of Cairo lie close to the Nile. Near the east bank is the main business section, as well as the Egyptian Museum and the Mugama'a, or government building. The Opera House/Cultural Center and the 590-foot (180-m) Cairo Tower stand on Gezira Island. To the northeast, a huge statue of Ramses II towers over the main railway station.

East of the city center is Khan al-Khalili *souq*, or market. Merchants have sold their wares there since the Fatimid

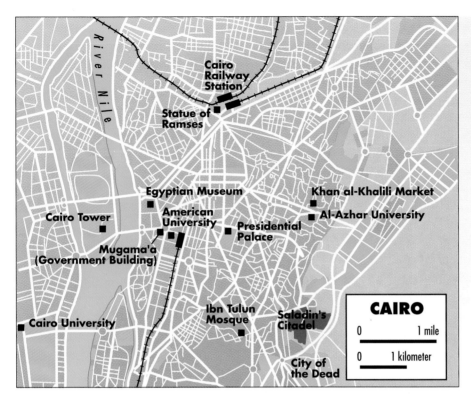

**Cairo:
Did You Know
This?**

Population: 6,800,000

Year founded: A.D. 969

Altitude: 420 feet (128 m)

**Average Daily
  Temperature:**
56°F (13°C) (January)
85°F (29°C) (July)

Average Annual Rainfall:

1 inch (2.5 cm)

dynasty in the 900s. South of the market are some of Egypt's grandest Islamic sites, including the Tulunid mosque of Ibn Tulun, the Ottoman mosque of Muhammad Ali, Saladin's Citadel, and the *madrasa* (religious school) of Mameluke Sultan Hassan.

Old Cairo, to the south, is the oldest section of town. It contains the Roman Fort of Babylon, the Coptic Museum, and many Coptic Christian churches.

Looming west of Cairo are the pyramids of Giza. They are close enough to be clearly seen from the windows of many Cairo office buildings.

Fruits of Their Labor

Egypt's economy has grown tremendously in the 1990s. Economic reforms have made Egypt the leading nation among the world's developing countries. The major reform program has been privatization—selling government-owned industries to private companies. Privatized industries become stronger and more flexible. They produce more and make more money. In the 1990s, the government sold power plants, roads, airports, banks, hotels, and many other businesses.

OTHER REFORMS HAVE INCLUDED IRRIGATING THE
Western Desert, building new cities, developing the
Mediterranean coastal strip, and building an underground
transit system.

Agriculture

Two of every five Egyptian workers make their living by farming. Many are small-scale farmers along the banks of the Nile.
They work the land by hand because their farms are too small
for large machines. By law, only an Egyptian can own farmland in Egypt.

Crops can grow on only about 4 percent of Egypt's land.
But water, plus year-round warm weather, makes the farms
highly productive. Almost all the farmland is in the Nile
Delta and the Nile River valley. Some desert regions are being
developed for farming. Other farmland is disappearing as
urban areas grow.

Egypt leads the world in producing long-staple (long-
fibered) cotton, its principal crop. The most important food
crops are grains such as rice, barley, wheat, and maize (corn).
Other important crops are onions, beans, tomatoes, and
oranges. Sugarcane and dates grow all year round.

Moving the Water

The *shadoof*, or water-
sweep, is a 4,000-year-old
method of drawing water
from a river. A long pole
with a weight on one end
is mounted on the bank. At
the other end is a goatskin
bag or bucket, which is
lowered into the water,
then swung onto the shore.

Egypt is the world's top producer of dates. In some fields, date palms are used as shade for other crops, such as cabbage. After the dates are harvested, they are spread out on the ground to dry.

Growing Seasons and Irrigation Methods

In ancient times, Egypt had two growing seasons. Now, thanks to the Aswan High Dam, farmers are able to plant three seasons of crops.

The summer season—from March to November—is the time for cotton, tomatoes, corn, rice, and potatoes. October through April is the main season, the time for growing wheat, barley, beans, onions, and bersim—a clover for animal feed. The

Egyptian workers sort through dates by hand.

Nile used to flood from July through October, but since the building of the Aswan Dam, that time is used as an extra growing season.

Pumping stations pump Nile water into wide irrigation canals along the bank. Smaller canals branch off from the main channel. Every three weeks, the canal gates are opened to flood the fields.

A gigantic irrigation project is planned for the Western Desert. It involves building a canal from the Nile to the New Valley oases. Irrigating the New Valley has been a dream since ancient times.

Money Facts

One Egyptian pound (£E) equals 100 piasters. There are 1-, 5-, 10-, 20-, and 100-pound bills, as well as 25- and 50-piaster bills.

Egyptian bank notes are printed in Arabic on one side and English on the other. Many show pictures of antiquities such as the temple at Abu Simbel, the mask of Tutankhamen, and statues of Ramses II. Others feature famous Islamic mosques.

What Egypt Grows, Makes, and Mines

Agriculture

Sugarcane	11,900,000 metric tons
Corn (maize)	4,883,000 metric tons
Tomatoes	4,600,000 metric tons

Manufacturing

Cement	17,430,000 metric tons
Nitrate fertilizers	5,437,000 metric tons
Reinforcing iron	1,681,000 metric tons

Mining

Iron ore	2,190,000 metric tons
Salt	972,000 metric tons
Clay	593,000 metric tons

Manufacturing

Egypt's most important industries are processed foods and cotton textiles. Textile plants spin cotton fibers into thread and yarn, weave cotton into cloth, and make finished clothing. Cotton yarn and fabric is Egypt's major export after petroleum products. Other manufactured goods include cements, chemicals, fertilizers, drugs, and steel.

This irrigated field in Saqqara lies beside a desert (and Djoser's step pyramid). Irrigation allows Egyptian farmers to grow crops throughout the year.

Nile Fishing

Fishing on the Nile is a culture of its own. Fishing families live and work on their boats. To catch fish from the boat, a child casts a net into the water as a grown-up rows. Then, as they drift around in a circular pattern, the net fills with fish.

In the past, the government built and owned most factories. This system is gradually changing. More and more factories are jointly owned by the government and private companies.

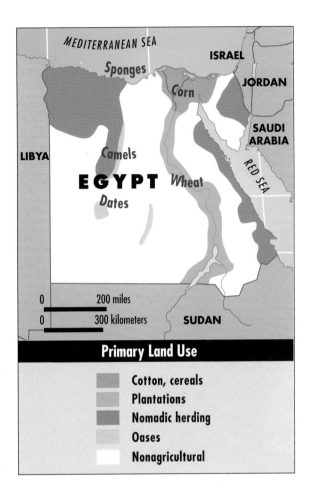

MEDITERRANEAN SEA

Sponges

ISRAEL

JORDAN

Corn

SAUDI ARABIA

LIBYA

Camels

EGYPT Wheat

RED SEA

Dates

0   200 miles

0   300 kilometers   **SUDAN**

Primary Land Use

Cotton, cereals
Plantations
Nomadic herding
Oases
Nonagricultural

Map of Egypt's natural resources

Mining

Thousands of years ago, Egypt's pharaohs used mining to increase their wealth. Gold, turquoise, and granite are among the treasures in Egypt's quarries and mines.

Today, petroleum and natural gas are Egypt's richest mineral resources. In the mid-1990s, Egypt was producing about one million barrels of oil a day. Petroleum products make up more than 40 percent of Egypt's exports.

Huge offshore oil rigs operate in the Gulf of Suez, Egypt's major oil-producing region. The Western Desert also has large natural gas and oil deposits. More oil and gas has been found near Giza and Port Said. Other important minerals include iron ore, phosphates, manganese, uranium, and coal.

Tourism

Tourism, one of Egypt's major sources of income, brings more than $4 billion into the country every year. Tourists pour into Egypt to see the Great Pyramid and the Sphinx. Around Luxor, they marvel at the Valley of the Kings and the temples of Karnak and Thebes. Near Aswan, they visit the Temples of Philae and Ramses II.

Cruises in "floating hotels" are popular, too. These luxurious boats take visitors up the Nile, stopping at ancient sites along the way. Tourist villages operate along the Red Sea coasts at Hurghada and in the Sinai.

In the early 1990s, extremist groups began attacking tourists. This was a blow for Egypt's tourism industry. Thanks to the government's stern antiterrorism measures, tourism is now recovering.

This mine in the Western Desert yields iron ore.

Buses, cars, and taxis—and sometimes donkey carts and camels—must share Cairo's busy streets.

Fewer than 2 percent of Egyptians own cars, although this may be hard to believe when you are driving in Cairo. City streets are thick with traffic. People also travel on buses, taxis, motorcycles, and bicycles. And even in Cairo, camels and donkey carts are part of the traffic flow.

With over 23,600 miles (38,000 km) of well-kept roads, travel throughout Egypt is easy. Signposts are in Arabic and English, and distances are shown in kilometers.

Roadways cover the Nile Valley and Delta. Others run along the Mediterranean and Red Sea coasts, out to the Western Desert oases, and through the Sinai. A major highway connects Cairo and Alexandria, while another runs alongside the Nile from Cairo to Aswan. A new loop highway circles around the New Valley oases.

To cross the Suez Canal, motorists drive underneath it in the Ahmad Hamdi road tunnel. But travelers must be sure and plan ahead. Traffic to the tunnel can be heavy, stalls are common, and the tunnel closes at night.

Egypt's main railway line runs from Alexandria to Aswan—almost the entire length of the country. From Cairo's Ramses Station, fast passenger trains take about $2\frac{1}{2}$ hours to Alexandria and 15 hours to Aswan.

Cairo's Metro, or underground railway system, was the first in Africa and opened in 1987. It has several stations in central Cairo and others in outlying areas. One Metro line goes through a tunnel under the Nile.

Water and Air Travel

Egyptians travel and transport goods on the Nile, just as their ancestors have done for thousands of years. Besides the 1,000-mile (1,600-km) river system, there are another 1,000 miles of canals. Passenger ferries sail between Egyptian ports and Italy, Greece, Cyprus, and Aqaba, Jordan.

Egyptian travelers wait for an underground train at Anwar Sadat Station.

Ferryboats carry passengers and vehicles of all kinds across the Nile between Luxor and Thebes every fifteen minutes.

For international trade, ships use the Mediterranean Sea, the Red Sea, and—connecting them—the Suez Canal. The canal is just over 100 miles (160 km) long. More than 17,000 ships pass through the Suez every year. Alexandria, on the Mediterranean, is the nation's major port. Others are Port Said and Damietta on the Mediterranean and Suez and Safraga on the Red Sea.

Most of the world's major airlines fly into Cairo's international airport at Heliopolis. Alexandria, Hurghada, and Nuzhah have international airports, too. Small airlines fly to many popular locations within the country.

Communications

Most of Egypt's publishing and broadcasting is centered in Cairo. The most important of the nation's fifteen daily newspapers are *Al-Ahram* (*The Pyramids*) and *Al-Akhbar* (*The News*). *Al-Jumhuriyah* (*The Republic*) is the government's official newspaper. *The Egyptian Gazette* and *Al-Ahram Weekly* are English-language papers.

Al-Ahram (*The Pyramids*) is one of Egypt's leading dailies.

About one of every three Egyptians owns a radio, and about one in ten has a TV set. The government owns Egypt's radio and television stations. That includes two national TV networks and regional stations in Cairo, Alexandria, and Ismailia. Satellites beam Egyptian programs to the rest of the Arab world, as well as to Great Britain and the United States. In hotels, guests can watch Cable News Network (CNN) for world news in English.

Except in the Western Desert oases, Egypt's telephone service is good. Major cities and towns have telephone centers where people can place local and international calls.

Crowded Cities, Common Bonds

Egypt has the second-highest population of all African nations, after Nigeria. In the mid-1990s, Egypt's population was estimated at more than 61 million. About 99 percent of Egypt's people live along the Nile or beside the Suez Canal, making these areas among the most densely populated in the world. Cairo and Alexandria are the largest cities. More than 15 million people live in the Cairo metropolitan area. Other densely populated cities are Giza and Port Said.

SMALL COMMUNITIES ARE CLUSTERED around the desert oases. The government is trying to attract more settlers to desert areas, but people keep moving to the cities for jobs and a better standard of living. There is a saying that, every minute in Cairo, one person is born and two arrive by train.

About 200,000 people live in the Sinai. Many are nomadic Bedouins who graze goats and sheep on the scrubby vegetation.

Bedouin women in ceremonial dress

Who Are the Egyptians?

Egyptians are classified as Hamitic people. As a rule, they think of themselves as Arabs, but there is no single Egyptian "type." Over the centuries, native Egyptians mixed with a staggering variety of people—Arabs, Berbers, Ethiopians, Persians, Turks, Central Asians, Greeks, and Romans. In the south, some have blended with the Nubians of northern Sudan.

Peasants who live in rural villages along the Nile are called *fellahin*. Many raise crops using the ancient methods and tools of their ancestors. The standard of living among the fellahin is low. Their average monthly income is less than fifty U.S. dollars.

Minority groups in Egypt include Copts, Bedouins, and Nubians. Among the many foreign nationals living in Egypt are British, Greek, and Italian people.

Population of Major Cities (1992 est.)

Cairo	6,800,000
Alexandria	3,380,000
Giza	2,144,000
Shoubra al-Kheima	834,000
Port Said	460,000

Who Lives in Egypt?

Egyptians
99%

Bedouins, Nubians, foreign nationals
(*Greeks, Italians, British*)
1%

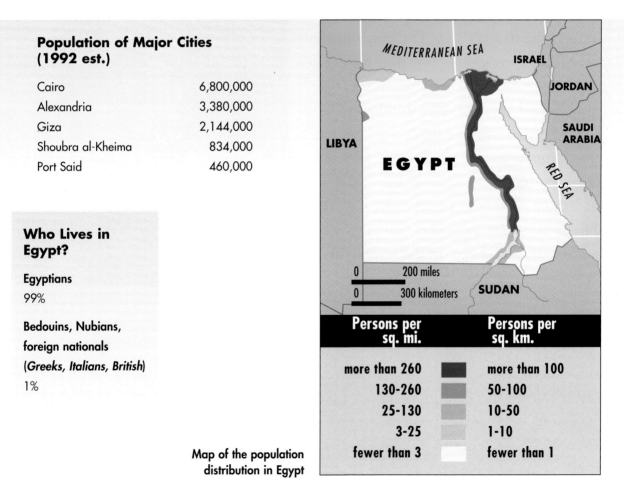

Map of the population distribution in Egypt

Persons per sq. mi.		Persons per sq. km.
more than 260		more than 100
130-260		50-100
25-130		10-50
3-25		1-10
fewer than 3		fewer than 1

Copts, Bedouins, and Nubians

Copts are not an ethnic minority, but a religious minority. They are direct descendants of Egyptians who lived in the days of the pharaohs. At the time of the Arab conquest, Copts formed the Christian majority. Over time, many converted from the Coptic Church to Islam. Today, some Copts are well-educated professionals, while others are wretchedly poor. The Egyptian government estimates that there are about two million Copts in Egypt, but the Copts themselves estimate their numbers at six to seven million.

A Nubian boy

Bedouins form a small minority of Egypt's population. They are traditionally a nomadic people, although many have settled down to a farming lifestyle. Bedouins were the original people of the Sinai, and most Sinai residents today are Bedouins. Others live in the Western and Eastern Deserts. Bedouins live throughout the Middle East—not only in Egypt, but also in Saudi Arabia, Jordan, and Israel. They think of themselves as

Bedouins and Arabs, rather than as citizens of one particular country.

Nubians are dark-skinned, non-Arabic people. Pharaohs of the Twenty-fifth Dynasty were Nubian kings. Traditionally, Nubians lived along the Nile south of Aswan and in northern Sudan. Many lost their homes when the Aswan High Dam was built. Some moved north, while others stayed in the Lake Nasser area.

Arabic Language and Writing

While Arabic is Egypt's official language, many Egyptians also speak English or French. The Arabic language has several forms. Classical Arabic is a complex language used in fine literature such as the Koran. Modern standard Arabic, which includes many new words taken from other cultures, is used in business and other official communications. At home or on the streets, people use local dialects. These can be very different from one region to another. The Cairene dialect is the most widespread.

Inshallah

Has the fever passed? *Inshallah* (insh-AH-lah). Will you get to Cairo tomorrow? *Inshallah*. Will the beans be ready by dinnertime? *Inshallah*. In Egypt, as in much of the Islamic world, many questions are answered with "*Inshallah*," meaning "God willing" or "If it pleases God." This expresses the belief that, regardless of our efforts, things happen only if God wills them.

Arabic Numbers

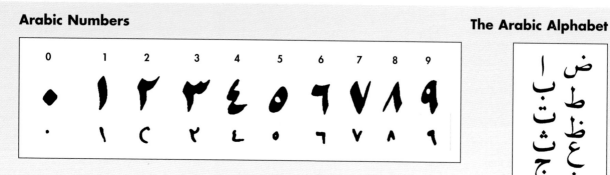

0	1	2	3	4	5	6	7	8	9
•	١	٢	٣	٤	٥	٦	٧	٨	٩
٠	١	٢	٣	٤	٥	٦	٧	٨	٩

The Arabic Alphabet

ض ط ظ ع غ ف ق ك ل م ن ه و ي ص ش س ز ر ذ د خ ح ج ث ت ب ا

Common Arabic Words and Phrases

yes	*aywa* (EYE-wah)	please	
no	*la*	(to a woman)	*minfadlik* (min-FAHD-lik)
hello	*assalaamu aleikum* (ah-sah-LA-moo ah-LAY-koom)	(to a man)	*minfadlak* (min-FAHD-lahk)
		thank you	*shukran* (shoo-KRAHN)
(response)	*wa aleikum assalaam* (WAH ah-LAY-koom ah-sah-LAHM)	no, thank you	*la shukran* (LA shoo-KRAHN)
good-bye	*ma salaama* (MA sah-LAH-mah)	Where is . . . ?	*Feyn . . . ?* (FAYN)
		How much?	*Bekaam?* (beh-KAHM)

Arabic script is based on the alphabet of an ancient people called the Nabataeans. It is written from right to left. Arabic writings can be so decorative that they are sometimes used as wall hangings and other art. The modern Arabic alphabet has twenty-eight characters (see above)—all consonants. Vowel sounds for *a*, *i*, and *u* are indicated by signs above or below a character. The digits used in the Western world—called Arabic numerals—are derived from Arabic numbers.

Coptic Language and Writing

The Coptic language comes from ancient Egyptian. It grew out of the language spoken there in the last 500 years B.C. At the time of the Arab invasion, Coptic was Egypt's everyday language. Then, for many years, both Arabic and Coptic were commonly spoken. But by the 1600s, spoken Coptic survived only in remote villages. The language is preserved today in Coptic Christian religious services.

Cairo is a metropolis that grows bigger every day.

Coptic writing had a history of its own. Ancient hieroglyphic writing changed into a script called *demotic*. When the Ptolemies came to power, Egyptians began writing the Coptic language with the Greek alphabet, adding seven demotic letters. In the 300s A.D., Copts translated the Bible from Greek into Coptic, and written Coptic took its final form. Coptic monks continue to preserve the script in prayer books.

Population Growth Problems

Egypt's population grows by about one million people every year. This creates problems of poverty, unemployment, housing shortages, and poor nutrition. However, between 1985 and 1995, Egypt's annual growth slowed from 3 percent to 2.2 percent. This was made possible by government programs for family planning and wider education about birth control. Conservative Islamic groups oppose efforts at family planning.

Government-subsidized housing complexes have been built on the outskirts of Cairo, but residents miss the hurly-burly of the city and its sense of community. Another program gives women 5 acres (2 ha) of desert land, along with a house and an income. The idea is that men will follow.

Feeding all the people is a major problem in overpopulated Egypt. Experts say that more farmland is now used to grow food for animals than food for people, due to a change in Egyptians' eating habits. Beef and chicken have become increasingly popular among middle- and upper-class Egyptians.

Population— A Worldwide Crisis

Between 1955 and 1987, the world population doubled—from 2.5 billion to 5 billion. Developing countries, including Egypt, account for about 90 percent of the world's population growth.

In 1994, the United Nations held its International Conference on Population and Development in Cairo. With Egypt's growing population, it was a fitting location. Conference members agreed on the key to population control: educating women and improving their status.

In 1997, Cairo hosted another international population conference. It studied the problem of how to balance population growth with natural resources.

People of God

Islam is Egypt's official religion, though people of other religions are free to practice their faith. About 90 percent of Egyptians follow Islam; most belong to the Sunni branch.

The Beautiful Names of God

In Islamic tradition, there are ninety-nine Beautiful Names of God. Muslims recite them, using prayer beads to keep count. Artists make paintings and wall hangings with the names in beautiful Arabic script. Arabic composers have also set the names to music.

ISLAM, MEANING "SUBMISSION," IS THE RELIGION OF THE entire Arab world. Its followers are *Muslim*, meaning "one who submits." Islam's central idea is monotheism—the belief in one God. For Muslims, God's name is Allah. A common Muslim prayer goes, "There is no God but God, and Allah is his name."

Muhammad, called the Prophet, was the founder of Islam. His teachings were written down in the Koran, Islam's holy book. Islamic teachings cover every aspect of daily life—food, clothing, education, and manners.

When Muslims worship in mosques, they leave their shoes at the door. The *muezzin* calls the faithful to prayer from the minaret, the mosque's tower. Five times a day, wherever they are, devout Muslims kneel to pray, facing the holy city of Mecca in Saudi Arabia. In most Islamic cities today, loud-speakers broadcast the call to prayer.

All faithful Muslims practice the Five Pillars of Faith: (1) believing in Allah as the one God and in Muhammad as his

Religions of Egypt

Sunni Muslims	90%
Shiite Muslims	3%
Coptic Christians	6%
Other Christian denominations	1%

Prophet; (2) praying five times a day, facing the holy city of Mecca; (3) giving aid to the needy; (4) fasting during the month of Ramadan; and (5) making a pilgrimage (*hajj*) to Mecca at least once.

The Islamic Calendar

Important Islamic Holidays

Ras al-Sana al-Hegira
(Islamic New Year)
Moulid an-Nabi
(Muhammad's birthday)
Ramadan
Aid al-Fitr (End of
Ramadan)
Aid al-Adha

Muslims divide the year into twelve months of twenty-nine or thirty days each, following cycles of the moon. Islamic astronomers determine the first day of each month. In different parts of the world, "first days" can be a day apart, because the moon is seen rising at different times.

The Islamic year is 354 days long (355 in leap years)—eleven days shorter than the Western, or solar, year. So each year, feast days fall eleven days earlier than in the year before.

"Year zero" in the Islamic calendar is A.D. 622. That was the year of the *hegira*, Muhammad's flight to Medina. Years are denoted A.H., or *anno hegirae*—the year of the hegira. For example, in much of the Middle East, the first day of the Islamic year A.H. 1419 is April 27, 1998, and A.H. 1420 begins on April 16, 1999.

Muhammad the Prophet

Born around A.D. 570, Muhammad was a merchant in the Arabian city of Mecca. At the time, the scattered tribes of Arabia had a variety of local gods, or *ilah*. One day, according to tradition, the angel Gabriel appeared to Muhammad in the desert. He told Muhammad to teach people to worship the one and only God, whose name is Allah. Merchants in Mecca were angered at Muhammad's teachings. In 622 they drove him out, and he fled to the city of Medina. His flight, called the *hegira*, is marked as the beginning of Islam.

Ramadan

During the month of Ramadan, Muslims celebrate Muhammad's receiving the Koran from God. All month long, they fast, taking neither food nor water from sunup to sundown. In Cairo, a cannon fires from Saladin's Citadel at sunset, announcing that it is time for *iftar*, the feast that breaks the fast.

A traditional *iftar* begins with dates and apricots. Next comes lentil soup, meat pies, vegetables, and finally, pastries. Feasting and parties go on through the night. Strings of lights and lanterns (*fanus*) brighten the streets, and boys shoot off firecrackers. At sunrise, the fasting begins again.

Men remove their shoes and kneel to pray during Ramadan, a month-long religious celebration.

Ramadan is also a time for exchanging good wishes and being especially generous to the poor. In some neighborhoods, tables are set up in the streets to feed poor people and travelers.

Coptic Christians

Coptic Christians form the largest religious minority in Egypt. They are the remnant of Egypt's Christian community before the Arab conquest.

Copts enjoy freedom of worship in Egypt but may not preach their religion to others. While Copts may convert to Islam, Muslims may not convert to the Coptic Church. In some areas, Copts have been targets of brutal attacks by Muslim extremists.

Saint Mark is believed to have brought Christianity to Egypt in the first century A.D. The new faith blended well with Egyptians' ancient beliefs, such as the final judgment and the importance of the afterlife. Christianity's first monasteries were set up in the deserts of Egypt. The first Christian monk, Saint Anthony, was a Copt.

A Muslim worshiper reads the Koran at a mosque in Old Cairo.

Easter, and the season of Lent before Easter, are the most important times in the religious calendar. During Lent, priests and monks fast from sunrise to sunset. Even after sunset, they have no meat, fish, eggs, wine, or coffee. The fast ends on Palm Sunday, a week before Easter. At the midnight service, the priests bless palm branches, which the people weave into crosses.

Copts have special reverence for the Holy Family—Jesus, Mary, and Joseph. Tradition holds that the Holy Family fled to Egypt to escape persecution. Coptic boys are baptized when they are forty days old, and girls are baptized at eighty days. Copts believe that the soul remains with the body for forty days after death.

The head of the Coptic Church—the Patriarch of Alexandria—oversees Coptic churches and monasteries throughout Egypt. The most famous historical churches are in Old Cairo on the ruins of the Roman fortress of Babylon. Several fourth-century Coptic monasteries stand at Wadi Natrun in the desert northwest of Cairo.

Important Coptic Holidays

Christmas

Epiphany

Easter

Pentecost

Coptic New Year

The Coptic Calendar

Roman emperor Diocletian executed thousands of Egyptian Christians. Copts mark the first year of his reign, A.D. 284, as the dawn of the "Era of Martyrs" and the beginning of their calendar. The Coptic year is based on the solar calendar, with twelve thirty-day months and extra days added at the end of the year. The Coptic calendar, also followed by farmers, is similar to the one used in ancient times.

Important Islamic Sites

Blue Mosque (*Mosque of Aqsunqur*) (Cairo) is famous for its indigo and turquoise tiles.

Citadel of Saladin (Cairo) is a fortress that encloses the Military Museum, Gawhara Palace, and several mosques, including that of Muhammad Ali.

Mosque of Amr ibn al-As (Cairo), built by Egypt's first Muslim conqueror in A.D. 642, is Egypt's oldest mosque.

Mosque of Ibn Tulun (Cairo) (top) built by the Tulunid prince Ahmed in 879, is Egypt's largest mosque.

Al-Azhar Mosque, built in 972, is Cairo's first Fatimid mosque. Its court is lined with marble columns and beautiful gypsum decorations.

Muhammad Ali Mosque (Cairo) (left) is also known as the Alabaster Mosque because of its alabaster-covered walls.

Mosque and Madrasa of Sultan Hassan (Cairo), built in 1356, is a Mameluke structure with marble paneling. Sherbet once flowed from its fountain for special occasions.

Important Coptic Sites

Cathedral of Saint Mark (Abbassia) is the largest cathedral in Africa and contains the remains of Saint Mark the Evangelist.

Church of Saint Mercurius (Cairo) contains Coptic art, including 175 icons of Old and New Testament scenes.

Church of Saint Sergius was built in the early 400s over the cave where the Holy Family took shelter on the flight to Egypt.

Church of the Virgin (Cairo) displays rare icons. Its wooden aisles are inlaid with ivory.

Church of the Virgin (Zaytoun) is famous for appearances of the Virgin Mary above one of its domes.

The **"Hanging Church,"** (right) built on top of the southern gate of Old Cairo's Fortress of Babylon, has three altars, a marble pulpit and pillars, and magnificent icons.

Monastery of Saint Anthony, near the Red Sea coast south of Suez, is dedicated to the early Christian hermit who lived and died there. Its library houses over 1,500 books, most in manuscript form.

Other Christian Sites

Church of Saint George (Old Cairo) is a Greek Orthodox church containing relics of Saint George.

Monastery of Saint Catherine, (bottom) at the foot of Mount Sinai, is a Greek Orthodox complex dating from the sixth century A.D. Its collections include several thousand manuscripts and icons, as well as many precious gold and jeweled objects.

The Ben Ezra Synagogue in Old Cairo houses many valuable historical and religious documents.

About one million Egyptians belong to other Christian groups. These include the Roman Catholic, Anglican, and Greek Orthodox churches.

A large Jewish community once flourished in Egypt. Jewish scholars translated many works of science and philosophy into Greek. They also translated the Bible's Old Testament from Hebrew into Greek. From this version, the *Septuagint*, translations were made into Coptic and Latin.

Today, a small minority of Jewish people—fewer than 2000—live in Egypt. The twelfth-century Ben Ezra Synagogue, in Old Cairo, is no longer used for worship. Tenth-century Hebrew documents were discovered there in the 1890s.

Arts, Culture, and Fun

Stand blindfolded in the bustling streets of Khan al-Khalili, and your nose will tell you where you are. Roses, cinnamon, and dozens of other sweet and savory smells fill the air. Merchants in this medieval Cairo bazaar are famous for their exotic perfumes and spices.

OTHER CRAFTSPEOPLE SELL HANDBLOWN GLASS, HAND-woven textiles, gold jewelry, and leather goods such as camel saddles. There are carved wooden boxes and trays inlaid with mother-of-pearl; brass and copper vases, cups, and trays; and statues made of alabaster, a cloudy white stone. Egypt's cotton fabrics are known for their beautiful colors and designs. Good-luck charms come in the form of the scarab beetle and the eye of Horus.

Down the highway south of Cairo, children are busy with needles and looms. They are learning to make traditional wall hangings and carpets at Wissa Wassef Art School in the village of Harraniyya. Their work is known around the world for its bold colors and playful designs.

These farm children contribute to the family income by weaving rugs after school.

Tomb Robbers

The Egyptian Museum in Cairo highlights 5,000 years of Egyptian history. Its vast collection includes treasures from Tutankhamen's tomb. In a special room of royal mummies, the preserved bodies of ancient pharaohs are displayed in glass cases.

Robbers have stolen much of the wealth of the pharaohs' tombs. In ancient times, people who built the tombs sometimes robbed them later. Ancient records have been found that describe a tomb robber's trial. A whole village in the Valley of the Kings once made its living by selling stolen

The renowned Egyptian Museum in Cairo displays the world's greatest collection of ancient Egyptian art.

Museum of Islamic Arts

The Museum of Islamic Arts in Cairo is the largest of its kind in the Middle East. It houses over 80,000 rare objects from Islam's beginnings through the Ottoman period, including coins, textiles, and ceramics. Its library contains rare Koran manuscripts, including one in Kufic script on gazelle skin.

Musicians play traditional instruments.

items from the valuable tombs. Egypt's Department of Antiquities does its best to crack down on the thefts, but it is still a problem.

Music and Performing Arts

Traditional Arabic instruments include the flute, oboe, viol, zither, and lute, as well as drums and tambourines. Popular songs tell tales of heartbreak and woe.

Umm Khulthum was Egypt's most beloved singer. More than three million grief-stricken fans joined her funeral procession in 1975. Today, Umm Khulthum Theater in Cairo hosts folk dances and other musical shows.

Cairo's Opera House, on Gezira Island at the end of At-Tahir Bridge, presents music and dance by Arabic artists. The Orchestra for Arabic Music often performs there.

Belly dancing is popular in much of the Middle East. While the most conservative Muslims frown on belly dancing, others see it as a fine art. In Egypt, belly dancers perform in hotels and nightclubs.

Literature and Films

Novelist Naguib Mahfouz (1911–), Egypt's greatest modern writer, has been called the inventor of the Arabic novel. His stories of Egyptian life earned him the 1988 Nobel Prize for Literature. In 1994, Islamic extremists tried to kill Mahfouz. They were protesting his use of God as a character in his novel *The Children of Gebelawi.*

Abbas al-Aqqad (1889–1964) is viewed as the greatest modern Arab poet. Even when he was imprisoned for political crimes, he continued to write deeply moving poetry.

Taha Hussein (1889–1973), minister of education from 1950 to 1952, was honored for his intellectual essays. Mahmoud Taymur (1894–1973) satirized Egyptian society in popular plays. Through essays and poems, Malak Hifni Nasif (1886–1918) tried to raise the status of Egyptian women.

Whirling Dervishes

Sufi is a branch of Islam known for its mystical practices. One group of Sufis seeks union with God through complex, spinning dances. The movements of these "whirling dervishes" are meant to imitate the paths of stars and planets whirling in the heavens. In Cairo, whirling dervishes perform twice a week at al-Ghuri Mausoleum.

The first Egyptian film was *The Civil Servant*, made in 1922. Since then, Egypt has produced every kind of film, from musical comedy to social realism. Censorship, severe at times, is more relaxed now. Today, Youssef Chahine and Mohamad Khan are two of Egypt's outstanding film directors.

Education

Forty-eight percent of Egypt's adult population can read and write—63 percent of Egyptian men and 34 percent of the women. Children must attend school from ages six through fourteen. Free public education is offered from primary grades through university level. About 10 million students are enrolled in Egypt's 20,000 primary and secondary schools.

Primary schools cover the first five grades, from ages six through eleven. Secondary schools last for six years, broken into two three-year cycles. About 91 percent of Egyptian children enter primary school, but about half the students drop out at age fourteen.

Graduates of Egyptian universities are well prepared for professional life. The nation has thirteen major universities and dozens of teachers' colleges.

Naguib Mahfouz

Naguib Mahfouz (1911–), an Egyptian novelist, writes in the Cairene dialect of Arabic. In 1988, he became the first Arabic-language writer to win the Nobel Prize for Literature. *Cairo Trilogy* is his most famous work.

Over 100,000 students are enrolled in Cairo University. Alexandria University is another important institution. Egypt's oldest university is the 1,000-year-old Al-Azhar University in Cairo—a major center of learning for the Islamic world.

Many of Egypt's schools are overcrowded and suffer from a lack of money, teachers, and school buildings. There is also a constant struggle between government authorities and religious zealots. "Islamists" want Islamic teachings to be part of every classroom subject. The government, on the other hand, wants nonreligious subjects to remain nonreligious.

Schoolgirls of the Delta region help each other with classwork.

Sports and Recreation

Soccer, or association football, is Egypt's national sport. Children play on school teams or in open fields. When professional soccer teams compete in Cairo for the annual derby, the city practically shuts down for the victory parties and parades.

Breeding, training, and racing horses is a long tradition in Egypt. During the Mameluke period, horsemanship became

The Alexandria Library Project

The Egyptian government and the United Nations Educational, Scientific, and Cultural Organization (UNESCO) are sponsoring a project to build a huge library in Alexandria. It will begin with a collection of 200,000 books and an International School of Information Studies. The idea was inspired by Alexandria's ancient library, built around 300 B.C.

Sailing on the Nile

a high art. The twelve classical skills included archery, swordsmanship, polo, and racing. Today there are riding and racing clubs in Cairo, Alexandria, and other cities.

Graceful white sails float along the Mediterranean, the Red Sea, and the Nile. They are either standard sailboats or *feluccas*—Egypt's traditional flat-bottomed boats. Windsurfing, waterskiing, rowing, and fishing are some other popular water sports. Rowers from around the world compete in the International Nile Rowing Competition. Egypt also hosts national and international fishing festivals every year.

The Red Sea is one of the world's best places for scuba diving and snorkeling. Its coral reefs are spectacular. Sharm el-Sheikh, on the Sinai Peninsula, is one of the finest locations. Other good diving spots are Ras Muhammad National Park, Dahab, Hurghada, and Safraga.

The Many Flavors of Life

For an Egyptian villager, food is simple and hearty. Most meals include a dish made with fava beans, or broad beans. People boil them for hours, often overnight, to make them soft enough to eat. In *ful*, the national dish, they are mixed with various herbs and spices for flavor. Sometimes beans are chopped and mixed with eggs. A ball or patty of soft beans is fried in olive oil to make *tamaiya*.

TAHINA IS A TASTY SESAME-SEED PASTE USED AS A DIP OR sandwich spread. When chickpeas, lemon juice, and garlic are added, it becomes *hummus*. *Babaganoush* is another dipping paste, made with eggplants and sesame. Cubes of veal or lamb's meat are often served on a skewer as *kebabs*. *Karkadé* is made with hibiscus flowers.

Aysh (Egyptian bread) is round and flat. It puffs up to make a handy pocket for meat or vegetables. Women bake bread in clay ovens, much as their ancestors did. Egyptians often use bread, instead of a spoon, to scoop up food.

Milk from cows, oxen, sheep, and goats is made into cheese. In rural areas, women fill a sheepskin or a goatskin with milk. They hang the skin up by strings and gently push it back and forth. In time, heat from the sun and acids from the skin ferment the liquid and it forms curds, or lumps of cheese.

Egyptians drink Turkish-style coffee—thick (almost muddy), black, and strong. People can choose to take it sweet, medium, or bitter. Tea, with sugar but no milk, is another popular drink.

What Kind of *Ful* Am I?

Egypt's national dish—*ful*—is especially popular as a breakfast food. There are as many versions of ful as there are cooks. To prepare ful, cook fava beans slowly for hours until soft. Mash garlic with sea salt and add lemon juice and olive oil. Stir this mixture in with the beans, along with chopped onions and parsley. Sprinkle with paprika and other savory spices. Serve with bread wedges, spring onions, and radishes.

A street vendor sells tamaiya, or felafel—patties of soft beans fried in oil.

Traditional Clothes

To wear the veil or not to wear the veil? In Egypt, a woman's dress style is a religious concern. Islamic law requires a woman to dress modestly. For conservative Muslims, this means wearing the *niqab*—a long dress and veil that shows only the eyes. Many women enjoy the comfort and privacy the niqab gives them in public. At home, among family and close friends, they may wear casual or even trendy clothes.

Less conservative women wear the *hijab*. It covers the body and the hair, but leaves the face uncovered. The hijab is popular because it honors Islamic law while making it easier to perform daily activities. Women doctors, professors, and engineers, as well as ordinary housewives, are seen wearing both styles of dress.

Many women consider themselves good Muslims, yet choose to dress in Western clothes. Some young women start out wearing Western clothes, then switch to "the veil" when they are older.

The traditional dress for Egyptian men is the *galabiyya*—a full-length, loose-fitting robe. Villagers wear the *baladi* style,

There are many styles of Muslim dress. These Muslim girls, for example, wear headscarfs of colorful material.

with a rounded neck and wide sleeves. *Saudi*-style robes are buttoned up to the neck. They fit more closely and the sleeves have cuffs. The *efrangi* style has a collar and cuffs like those on Western dress shirts. Many men wear a traditional Arabic checked scarf wrapped around the head like a turban. Some wear the typical Islamic skullcap.

Egyptian men in traditional robes and turbans

A Community Built on Garbage

Mokattam, a slum on the east edge of Cairo, is the city's garbage dump. It is also home to the *zabaleen* (garbage collectors) and their families. Garbage is everywhere in Mokattam—in the streets, on the rooftops, and against the houses. For children, playing means playing in garbage heaps.

Each day, about 2,000 tons (1,814 metric tons) of garbage arrive at the dump. Then the sorting begins. People pick out glass, plastic, and metal for recycling. Men and boys forge metal into car parts and other items they can sell to factories. Women and girls find scraps of cloth to make into clothes and rugs.

The residents' efforts are paying off. They have built new businesses and roads and hired doctors and nurses for their hospital.

Housing: Bursting at the Seams

In Cairo and Alexandria, most people live in apartment buildings. Apartments range from palacelike to closet-size. Most are rented, although some may be owned by the resident. In a new complex in Cairo, apartments are said to cost up to several million dollars. In finer suburbs, single-family houses may have marble floors with hot-water pipes beneath the floors for warmth.

Cairo does not have enough housing for its growing population. People live and sleep wherever they can—on rooftops, in garbage dumps, or on boats. Parents, grandparents, and children often live in tiny, two- or three-room apartments. "If you fainted," some like to say, "you would not fall down."

Some people have even set up homes in cemeteries. A district of sultans' tombs on the east edge of Cairo is known as the "City of the Dead." More than 100,000 people live there. Residents have their own schools, shops,

In Old Cairo, space is so tight, apartment buildings butt against historic buildings.

Wall paintings depicting a pilgrimage to Mecca

and mosques. Even some middle-class people live in the City of the Dead. They find it quieter and less crowded than the city center.

Rural peasants—the *fellahin*—live in one-story houses with flat roofs made of straw or palm wood. The thick walls are made of mud or sun-baked mud bricks. In hot weather, the roof is a cool place to sleep.

Many houses have dirt floors and no electricity or running water. People sit on mats or benches around a low table. Some people paint their houses with blue trim to ward off evil. Those who have made a pilgrimage to Mecca paint scenes from their trip on the outside walls.

Festival Time

The month of Ramadan is Egypt's most festive season. Other holidays are the *moulids*—festivals honoring a holy person. Moulid an-Nabi, Muhammad's birthday, is celebrated across the Islamic world. In Cairo, a fantastic procession surges through the streets, and the night is ablaze with lights. Each town also celebrates the moulid of its own patron saint. On July 14, Coptic Christians gather at the White Monastery near Sohag for Saint Shenute's moulid.

Sham an-Nessim is the day people throw open the windows and take a deep breath. This springtime "fresh air" holiday falls on the Monday after Coptic Easter. Sham an-Nessim means "breathing in the breeze." Families enjoy picnics and eat salt fish, onions, and colored eggs.

A farmer sits with his children after a breakfast of ful and Egyptian bread.

Village Life

Most of the fellahin are farmers living in small villages along the Nile, as their ancestors did thousands of years ago. Some own their land, while others rent land or work for landowners.

Villagers eat breakfast at about 6 A.M. before starting to work. Boys take the sheep and goats out to graze. When they are older, their fathers teach them traditional farming methods. Women bake

A peasant woman bakes traditional Egyptian bread in an outdoor clay oven.

bread in outdoor ovens. Girls milk goats, feed chickens, and fetch water from the village well, balancing baskets, water jars, or stacks of bread on their heads. The workday ends at sundown, and everyone gathers for the evening meal of rice, vegetables, and ful.

City Life

A young boy sells magazines that he has fished out of a garbage bin. His father shines shoes, and his mother sells bread. About 20 percent of the people in Cairo are unemployed. Those who work may be executives, clerks, factory workers, shopkeepers, or street merchants. Child labor is illegal, but many children work long hours to help their families survive.

Almost half of all Egyptians live in urban areas. Villagers who can no longer survive on farms pour into the cities every day. Many bring their goats and chickens along. The first surprise they get is air pollution. Cairo's levels of dust and lead are among the highest in the world.

A busy Cairo street

Cairo's public buses are packed, and traffic is thick and wild. Drivers are aggressive and seem to make up their own rules. However, everyone seems to understand the system, and accidents are rare.

Those who can afford it leave Cairo on weekends and in the hot summer months. Many go to Alexandria or to other Mediterranean cities, where they enjoy cool sea breezes, cleaner air, less noise, and more room.

In the cities, people eat breakfast around 7:30 A.M. Lunch is in mid-afternoon, and dinner is served at 10 P.M. or later. Many shops and businesses close for a two- or three-hour midday break. For Muslims, Friday is the holy day of the week, and many businesses close or have shorter hours on this day.

Egyptian men enjoy getting together in cafés to drink Turkish coffee, play backgammon, and smoke water pipes. People from all walks of life like to relax in outdoor cafés where they can sit back and watch the vibrant life of the city around them.

Sidewalk vendors sell live chickens, papyrus paintings, and sweets. Cars and bicycles swerve around long-robed men guiding donkey carts. Women scurry through the maze, balancing jars or platters on their heads. Even in narrow alleys, people seem to follow unspoken "rules of the road." Maybe they know that, if they give an inch here and there, everyone gets what they need.

Opposite: **A Muslim woman balances a cage of birds on her head.**

Timeline

	World's History		**Egypt's History**	
The Renaissance begins in Italy.	1300s			
The Black Death sweeps through Europe.	1347			
Ottoman Turks capture Constantinople, conquering the Byzantine Empire.	1453			
Columbus arrives in North America.	1492			
The Reformation leads to the birth of Protestantism.	1500s	1517	Ottoman Turks invade Egypt and rule for almost 300 years.	
The Declaration of Independence is signed.	1776	1798	Napoleon conquers Egypt.	
The French Revolution begins.	1789			
The American Civil War ends.	1865	1869	The Suez Canal is completed.	
		1882	Britain occupies Egypt.	
World War I breaks out.	1914	1914	Britain declares Egypt a protectorate.	
The Bolshevik Revolution brings Communism to Russia.	1917	1922	Britain grants Egypt nominal independence.	
Worldwide economic depression begins.	1929			
World War II begins, following the German invasion of Poland.	1939			
The Vietnam War starts.	1957	1952	King Farouk is dethroned.	
		1953	Egypt is declared a republic.	
		1956	Gamel Abdel Nasser is elected president; Nasser takes control of Suez Canal.	
		1967	Israel occupies the Sinai in the Six-Day War.	
		1973	Egypt and Israel clash in the October War.	
		1978	Anwar Sadat and Menachem Begin of Israel sign the Camp David Accords.	
		1981	Anwar Sadat is assassinated; Hosni Mubarak becomes president.	
The Berlin Wall is torn down, as Communism crumbles in Eastern Europe.	1989	1990	Egypt emerges as a Middle East leader after the Iraqi invasion of Kuwait.	
Bill Clinton is reelected U.S. president.	1996			

Fast Facts

Official name: Arab Republic of Egypt

Cairo

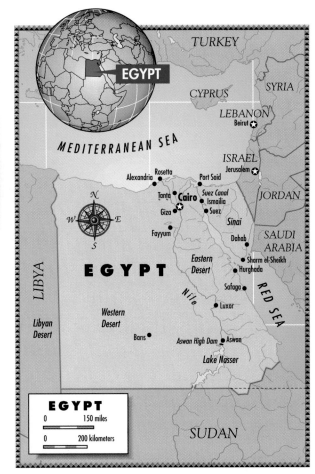

Capital: Cairo

Official language: Arabic

Flag of Egypt

President Hosni Mubarak

Official religion: Islam

Year of founding: Menes, the first pharaoh, united Egypt in about 3100 B.C. In 1922, Egypt became an independent nation. In 1953, Egypt became a republic.

Founder: Gamal Abdel Nasser is considered the father of the Egyptian republic.

National anthem: "*Beladi, Beladi*," meaning "my country, my country"

Government: Republic with one legislative house

Chief of state: President

Head of government: Prime minister

Area and dimensions: Egypt covers 386,662 square miles (1,001,450 sq km). The country stretches 675 miles (1,086 km) north to south and 770 miles (1,239 km) east to west.

Land and water borders: Egypt is bordered by Mediterranean Sea to the north, Sudan to the south, Libya to the west, and the Red Sea, Gulf of Aqaba, and Israel to the east.

Highest elevation: *Jabal Katrinah* (Mount Saint Catherine), 8,651 feet (2,637 m)

Lowest elevation: Qattara Depression, 436 feet (133 m) below sea level

Average temperatures:	in January	in July
Cairo	56°F (13°C)	85°F (29°C)

Average annual rainfall:		
Alexandria	7 inches (18 cm)	
Aswan	0.1 inch (0.25 cm)	

National population (1997 est.): 61,500,000

Population (1992 est.)
of largest cities in Egypt:

Cairo	6,800,000
Alexandria	3,380,000
Giza	2,144,000
Shoubra al-Kheima	834,000
Port Said	460,000

Famous landmarks:

▶ The Great Pyramids and the Sphinx (Giza)

▶ Luxor Temple and Museum, Temple of Karnak, and the Valleys of the Kings (Luxor)

▶ Aswan High Dam and Lake Nasser (Aswan)

▶ Abu Simbel and Temple of Ramses II (southern Egypt near the border with Sudan)

▶ Qaytbey Fort, Pompey's Pillar, Kom al-Shogafa Catacombs, Anfushi and Chatby Tombs, Ras al-Tin Palace, Kom al-Dikka Amphitheater, and the Greco-Roman Museum (Alexandria)

▶ Djoser's step pyramid and funeral complex (Saqqara)

▶ The Suez Canal and some of Egypt's best beaches (Port Said, Ismailia)

▶ Colossus of Ramses II, Mummification Beds of Apis Bulls, and Temple of Ptah (Memphis)

Industry: Food processing is the largest industry in Egypt, thanks to its huge output of refined sugar, with cotton yarn and cured tobacco also high on the list. Producing fertilizer for Egypt's crops is another major industry, as is the manufacturing of tractors, cars, and household appliances.

The Great Pyramid

Currency:	One Egyptian pound (£E) equals 100 piasters. 1997 exchange rate: US$1=£E3.33
Weights and measures:	Metric system
Literacy:	48.4%

Common Arabic words and phrases:

assalaamu aleikum (ah-sah-LA-moo ah-LAY-koom)	hello
aywa (EYE-wah)	yes
baksheesh (bak-SHEESH)	alms, or money given to the poor
Bekaam? (beh-KAHM)	How much?
Feyn . . . ? (FAYN)	Where is . . . ?
hijab (hee-ZHAHB)	a long dress with a veil covering the hair
la (LA)	no
ma salaama (MA sah-LAH-mah)	good-bye
moulid (moo-LEED)	a festival to celebrate a religious event
niqab (nee-KAHB)	a long dress and veil that exposes only the eyes
sheikh (SHAKE or SHEEK)	an Arab chief
shukran (shoo-KRAHN)	thank you
souq (SOOK)	a marketplace
wadi (WAH-dee)	a dry riverbed that has become a trail or valley

To Find Out More

Nonfiction

▶ Giblin, James C. *The Riddle of the Rosetta Stone.* New York: HarperCollins, 1990.

▶ Harik, Ramsay M., and Elsa Marston. *Women in the Middle East: Tradition and Change.* Danbury, CT: Franklin Watts, 1996.

▶ Harris, Geraldine. *Gods and Pharoahs from Egyptian Mythology.* New York: Peter Bedrick, 1992.

▶ Hart, George. *Ancient Egypt.* New York: Random House, 1990.

▶ Lerner Geography Department Staff. *Egypt in Pictures.* Minneapolis: Lerner Publications, 1988.

▶ Macaulay, David. *Pyramid.* Boston: Houghton Mifflin, 1975.

▶ Morrison, Ian A. *Egypt.* Chatham, NJ: Raintree Steck-Vaughn, 1991.

▶ Reeves, Nicholas. *Into the Mummy's Tomb: The Real-Life Discovery of Tutankhamun's Treasures.* New York: Scholastic, 1992.

▶ Scott, Joseph, and Lenore Scott. *Egyptian Hieroglyphs for Everyone: An Introduction to the Writing of Ancient Egypt.* New York: HarperCollins, 1990.

▶ Steele, Philip. *The Egyptians and the Valley of the Kings.* New York: Dillon Press, 1994.

Biographies

▶ Green, Robert. *Tutankhamun.* Danbury, CT: Franklin Watts, 1996.

▶ Stanley, Diane. *Cleopatra.* New York: Morrow Junior Books, 1994.

▶ Sullivan, George. *Sadat: The Man Who Changed Mid-East History.* New York: Walker, 1981.

Videotapes

▶ *Egypt: Quest for Eternity.* National Geographic Society, Columbia Tristar Home Video, 1993.

▶ *Mummies Made in Egypt.* Lincoln, NE: Great Plains National Instructional Television Library, 1988.

CD-ROMs

▶ *Nile: Passage to Egypt.* Bethesda, MD: Discovery Communications, 1995.

Websites

▶ **Consulate of Egypt**
http://www-ceg.ceg.uiuc.edu/
~haggag/consulate.html
Provides information on Egyptian culture, history, sports, news, and archaeological sites.

▶ **Institute of Egyptian Art and Archeology**
http://www.memphis.edu/egypt/
egypt.html
Takes you on a short color tour of ancient Egyptian sites.

▶ **Hieroglyphic Alphabet**
http://www.idsc.gov.eg/tourism/
tor_trn.htm
Provides hieroglyphic versions of various words.

Organizations and Embassies

▶ **Embassy of the Arab Republic of Egypt**
2310 Decatur Place NW
Washington, DC 20008
(202) 234-3903

▶ **Egyptian Tourist Authority**
630 Fifth Avenue, Suite 1706
New York, NY 10111
(212) 332-2570

Index

Page numbers in *italics* indicate illustrations

Meet the Author

ANN HEINRICHS FELL IN LOVE WITH FARAWAY PLACES while reading Doctor Dolittle books as a child. She has traveled through most of the United States, several countries in Europe, Morocco, the Middle East, and east Asia. Her experiences in Egypt were the backdrop for this book.

On her trip to Egypt she visited pyramids and tombs, climbed Mount Sinai, and camel-trekked in the desert. "Don't believe what people say about mean-tempered camels. They are the sweetest, smartest animals alive," she says.

"Trips are fun, but the real work—tracking down all the factual information for a book—begins at the library. I head straight for the reference department. My favorite resources include United Nations publications, world almanacs, and the library's computer databases.

"To me, writing nonfiction is a bigger challenge than writing fiction. With nonfiction, you can't just dream something up; everything has to be researched. I study government

reports, analyze statistics tables, then try to give the information a human face. And I'm always looking for what kids in the other country are up to, so I can report back to kids here.

"For this book, I also read several weeks' worth of Egyptian newspapers. They told me about day-to-day issues and problems. The Egyptian consulate and Egyptologists at a local university provided more information."

Ann Heinrichs grew up in Arkansas and lives in Chicago. She is the author of more than twenty books for children and young adults on American, Asian, and African history and culture. (*Tibet*, in the first Enchantment of the World series, was awarded honorable mention by the National Federation of Press Women.) Ann Heinrichs has also written numerous newspaper, magazine, and encyclopedia articles. She holds a bachelor's and master's degree in piano performance. These days, her performing arts are t'ai chi, nan chuan, and kung fu sword.

Photo Credits